Senses

How we connect with the world

Contributors

Author: Francesca Baines BA is an editor and writer for adults and children on topics ranging from transport to psychology. She specializes in writing for children on scientific subjects.

Series consultant: Richard Walker BSc PhD PGCE taught biology, science, and health education for several years before becoming a full-time writer. He is a foremost author and consultant specializing in books for adults and children on human biology, health, and natural history. He is the author of *Heart: How the blood gets around the body, Making Life: How we reproduce and grow, Muscles: How we move and exercise,* and *Brain: Our body's nerve center* in this series and is consultant on the whole series

Advisory panel

1 Heart: How the blood gets around the body
P. M. Schofield MD FRCP FICA FACC FESC is Consultant Cardiologist at Papworth Hospital, Cambridge, UK

2 Skeleton: Our body's framework
R. N. Villar MS FRCS is Consultant Orthopedic Surgeon at Cambridge BUPA Lea Hospital and Addenbrooke's Hospital, Cambridge, UK

3 Digesting: How we fuel the body
J. O. Hunter FRCP is Director of the Gastroenterology Research Unit, Addenbrooke's Hospital, Cambridge, UK

4 Making Life: How we reproduce and grow
Jane MacDougall MD MRCOG is Consultant Obstetrician and Gynecologist at the Rosie Maternity Hospital, Addenbrooke's NHS Trust, Cambridge, UK

5 Breathing: How we use air
Mark Slade MA MBBS MRCP is Senior Registrar, Department of Respiratory Medicine, Addenbrooke's Hospital, Cambridge, UK

6 Senses: How we connect with the world
Peter Garrard MA MRCP is Medical Research Council Fellow and Honorary Specialist Registrar, Neurology Department, Addenbrooke's Hospital, Cambridge, UK

7 Muscles: How we move and exercise
Jumbo Jenner MD FRCP is Consultant, and
R. T. Kavanagh MD MRCP is Senior Registrar, Department of Rheumatology, Addenbrooke's Hospital, Cambridge, UK

8 Brain: Our body's nerve center
Peter Garrard MA MRCP is Medical Research Council Fellow and Honorary Specialist Registrar, Neurology Department, Addenbrooke's Hospital, Cambridge, UK

Senses

How we connect with the world

Francesca Baines

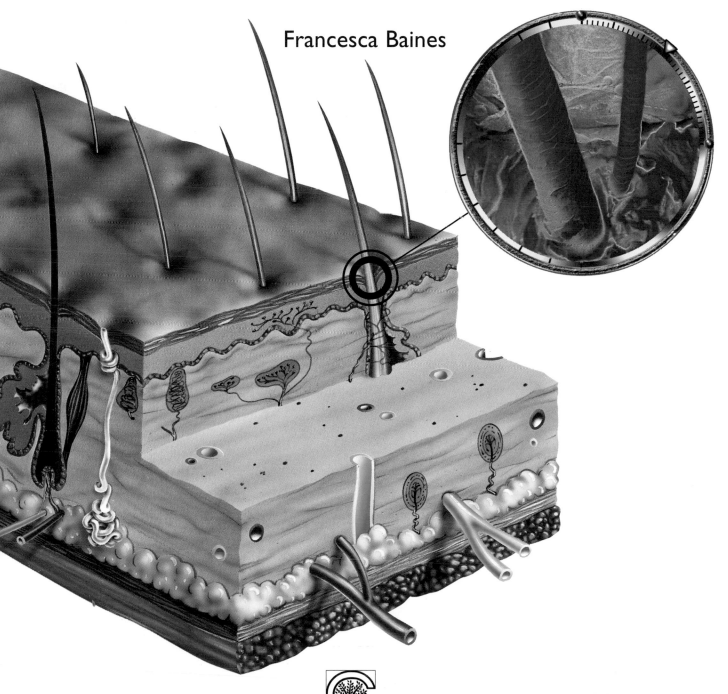

GROLIER EDUCATIONAL

SHERMAN TURNPIKE, DANBURY, CONNECTICUT 06816

ABOUT THIS BOOK

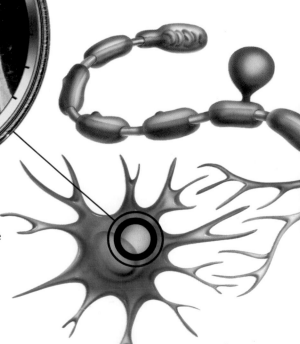

Under the Microscope uses microphotography to allow you to see right inside the human body.

The camera acts as a microscope, looking at unseen parts of the body and zooming in on the body's cells at work. Some microphotographs are magnified hundreds of times, others thousands of times. They have been dramatically colored to bring details into crisp focus and are linked to clear and accurate illustrations that fit them in context inside the body.

New words are explained the first time that they are used and can also be checked in the glossary at the back of the book, which includes a helpful pronunciation guide.

First published in 1998 by
Grolier Educational
Sherman Turnpike
Danbury
Connecticut

Set ISBN 0-7172-9265-7
Volume ISBN 0-7172-9270-3

Library of Congress Cataloging-in-Publication Data

Under the microscope : the human body
    p.   cm.
  Includes bibliographical references and index
  Contents: v. 1. Skeleton - v. 2. Brain - v. 3. Heart - v. 4. Making life - v. 5. Senses - v. 6. Digesting - v. 7. Muscles - v. 8. Breathing.
  ISBN 0-7172-9265-7 (set)
  1. Human physiology - Juvenile literature.
2. Human anatomy - Juvenile literature.
3. Body. Human - Juvenile literature. [1. Human physiology. 2. Human anatomy.
3. Body, Human.]
I. Grolier Educational (Firm)
QP37,U53 1998
612–DC21
97-38977
CIP
AC

Produced by Franklin Watts
96 Leonard Street
London EC2A 4RH

Creative development by
Miles Kelly Publishing
Unit 11
The Bardfield Centre
Great Bardfield
Essex CM7 4SL

Printed in Belgium

Designed by Full Steam Ahead

Illustrated by Janos Marffy

Artwork commissioned by
Branka Surla

Picture research by Elaine Willis

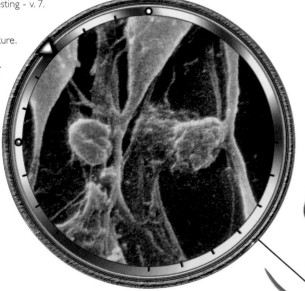

Nerve cells
Messages are sent from the sensory organs to the brain, the body's control center, along nerve cells called neurons. Two neurons are shown on the right, a long sensory neuron and a round, spiky association neuron. Association neurons (above) are found in the spinal cord and in the brain.

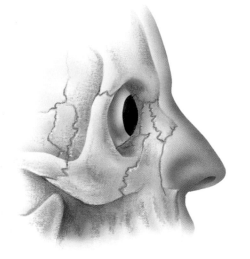

CONTENTS

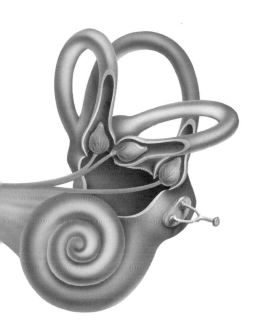

Introduction	6
Senses & the Nervous System	8
The Skin	10
Feeling	12
Protecting the Body	14
Body Temperature	16
Taste	18
Smell	20
The Ear	22
Hearing	24
Distinguishing Sounds	26
Balance on the Move	28
Which Way Up?	30
The Eye	32
Focusing Light	34
How the Eye Works	36
Visual Pathways	38
How We See	40
Vision Problems	42
Animal Vision	44
Glossary	46
Set Index	47

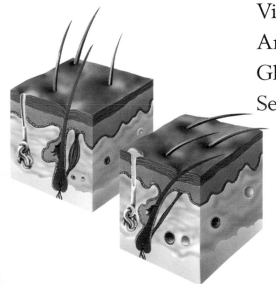

INTRODUCTION

Taste
Sensors on your tongue, called taste buds, respond to the different tastes in foods. Taste and smell work together to give you the flavor of the food you eat.

You know about the world around you only because your body has senses. There are five main senses — touch, smell, taste, hearing, and sight. These are known as your external sensory system because they tell you about the world outside your body.

You also have an internal sensory system that tells you what is happening inside your body — for example, when you are hungry, thirsty, tired, or in pain.

Most external sense organs — your eyes, ears, nose, and tongue — are in your head; touch sensors are located in the skin. Each of these organs responds to changes in your surroundings called stimuli. A stimulus could be a change in light, a sound, or a food flavoring. Stimuli cause sensors to send signals to the brain. The brain sorts out these signals into something we become aware of and understand, such as a sight, a sound, or a taste. The information provided by senses is important because it helps us protect ourselves and enjoy a world of sights, sounds, flavors, and smells.

Smell
As you breathe in through your nose, the tiny hairlike structures called cilia shown here are able to detect smells in the air.

Sight
Your eyes respond to light and send messages to your brain so that you can see the world around you. The iris (right) gives the eye its color.

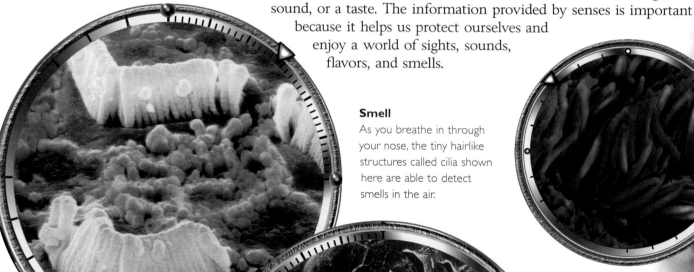

Sound
Deep inside your ear are the tiny sound-sensitive hairs of the organ of Corti, shown above. Without them you would not be able to enjoy listening to music or to your friends talking.

Touch
You feel things because your body is covered in sensitive skin. Here you can see the tough outer covering of the skin. Below this lies a bank of sensors that detect touch, heat, cold, and pain.

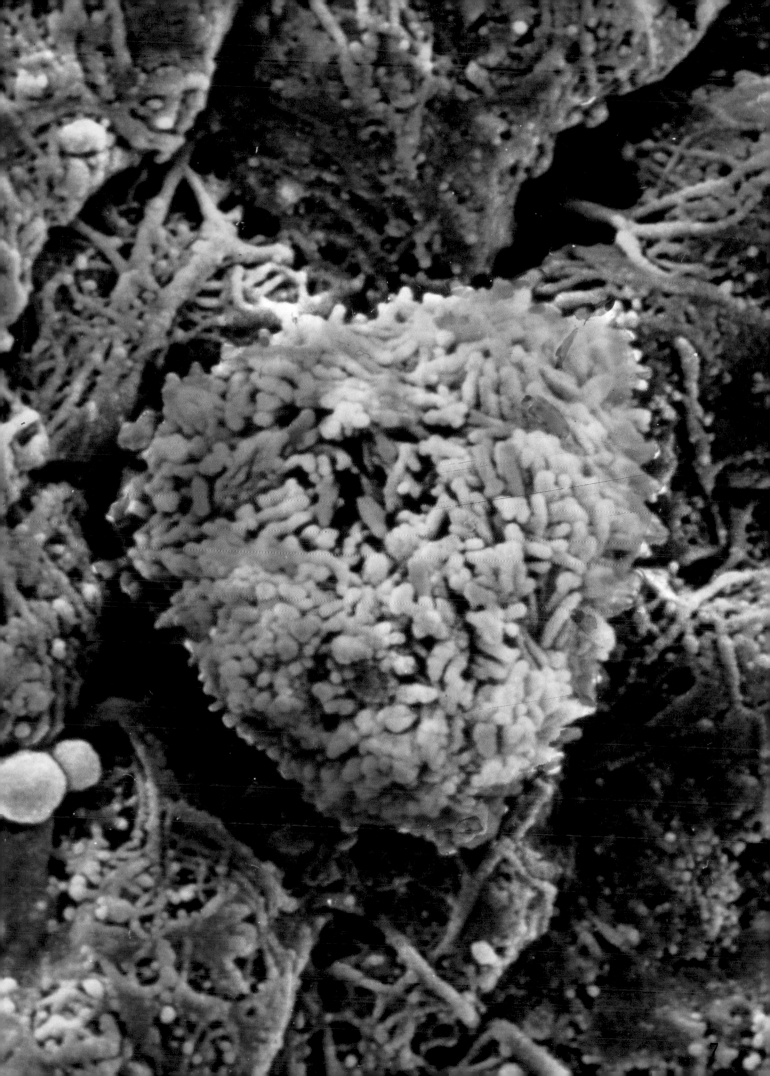

SENSES & THE NERVOUS SYSTEM

Your body's sense organs constantly send signals about what is happening outside and inside it to the body's control center — the brain. The parts of the sense organ that receive information are called the receptor cells.

Each receptor cell responds to a particular stimulus — such as bright light, a hot object, or a high-pitched sound. The brain is able to control the body because it is linked to receptor cells all over the body by a network of long thin cells — called neurons — that carry electrical signals. These signals are called nerve impulses. Neurons are bundled together into nerves rather like electric cables. Nerves relay nerve impulses between the brain and all parts of the body.

The route to the brain
Signals from receptors in your skin travel first to a column of nervous tissue called the spinal cord that runs inside your backbone. Most information passes in and out of the brain along the spinal cord. Information from sensory organs in your head goes straight to the brain.

How soft is this bear?
Stroking a teddy bear triggers many different receptor cells to give you a lot of information about what you are doing. Some receptor cells detect the gentle pressure of stroking something soft, some tell you that you are stroking something furry, and others that you are in contact with something warm.

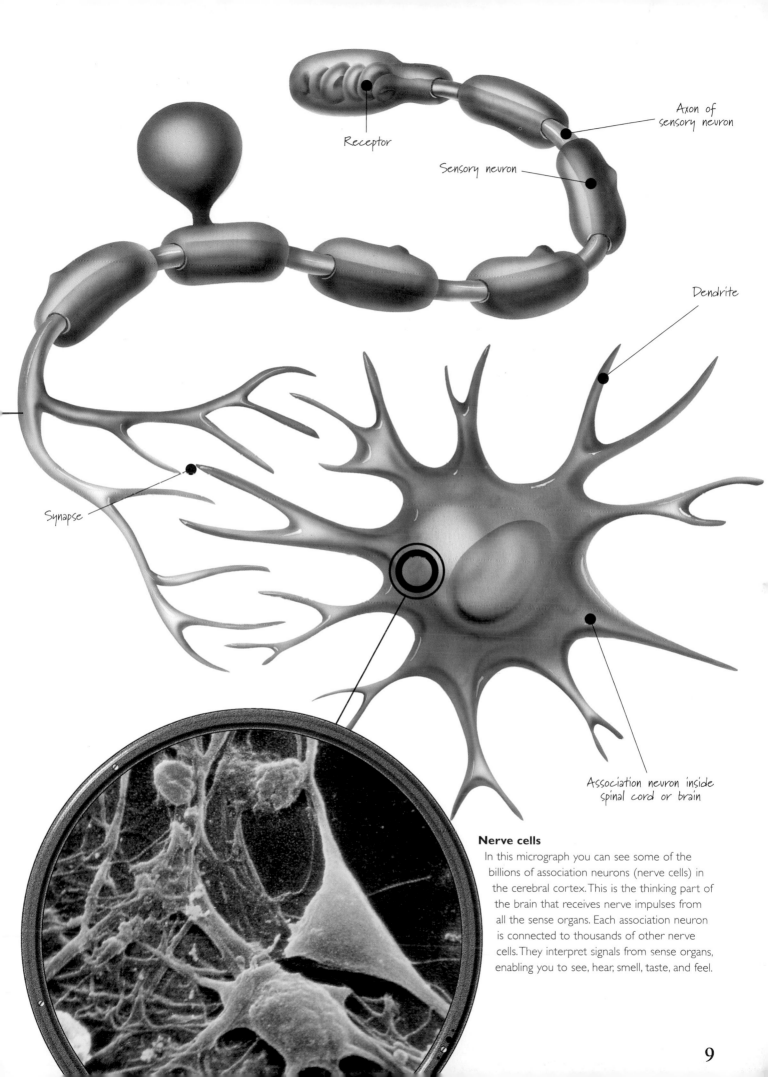

Axon of
sensory neuron

Receptor

Sensory neuron

Dendrite

Synapse

Association neuron inside
spinal cord or brain

Nerve cells

In this micrograph you can see some of the
billions of association neurons (nerve cells) in
the cerebral cortex. This is the thinking part of
the brain that receives nerve impulses from
all the sense organs. Each association neuron
is connected to thousands of other nerve
cells. They interpret signals from sense organs,
enabling you to see, hear, smell, taste, and feel.

THE SKIN

Your body is sensitive to touch, heat, cold, and pain because the skin is packed with sensors. Skin is the body's largest organ. It also waterproofs the body, protects it from injury and infection, and helps control your body's temperature.

The outer layer of the skin is called the epidermis. Its upper part is dead and is continuously wearing away. Beneath the epidermis is a living layer called the dermis. The skin's sense receptors are found in the dermis, along with blood vessels and sweat glands. Most of your skin is covered with hairs that grow from pits in the dermis. Hairs help your sense of touch. The hairs are dead, except for a small part just above the base. But at their roots they have sense receptors that are stimulated when the hair is touched. Nails protect the sensitive ends of your fingers and toes. Hairs, nails, and the outer epidermis contain a tough material called keratin.

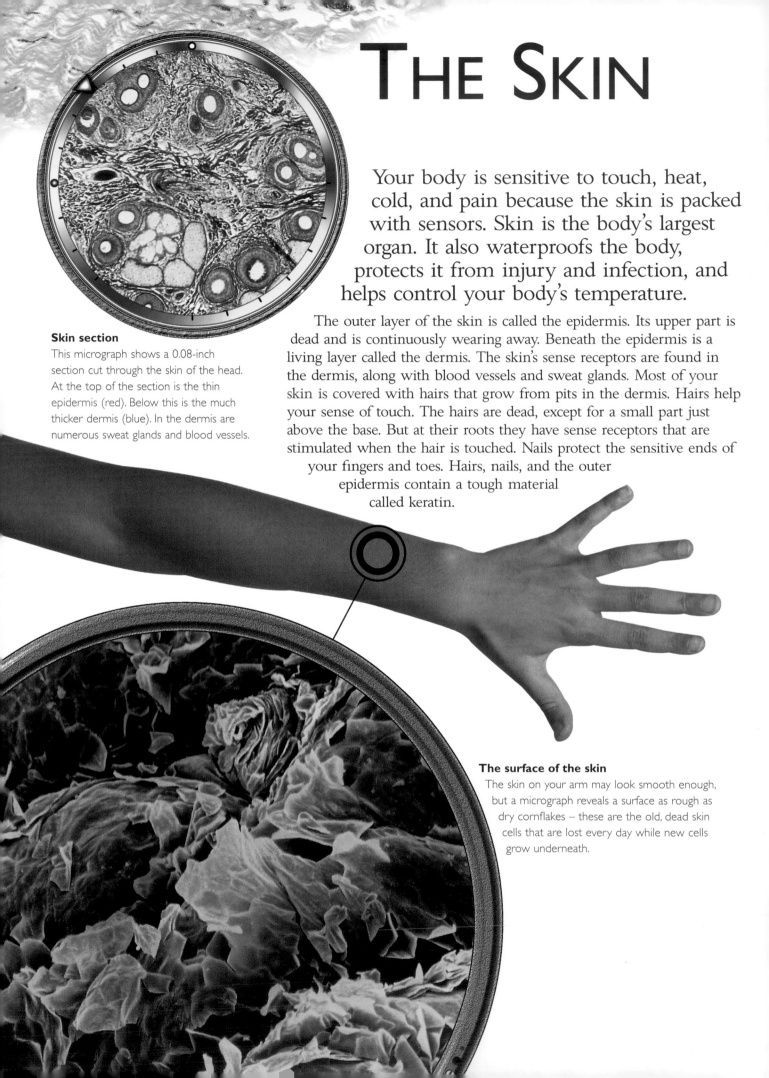

Skin section
This micrograph shows a 0.08-inch section cut through the skin of the head. At the top of the section is the thin epidermis (red). Below this is the much thicker dermis (blue). In the dermis are numerous sweat glands and blood vessels.

The surface of the skin
The skin on your arm may look smooth enough, but a micrograph reveals a surface as rough as dry cornflakes – these are the old, dead skin cells that are lost every day while new cells grow underneath.

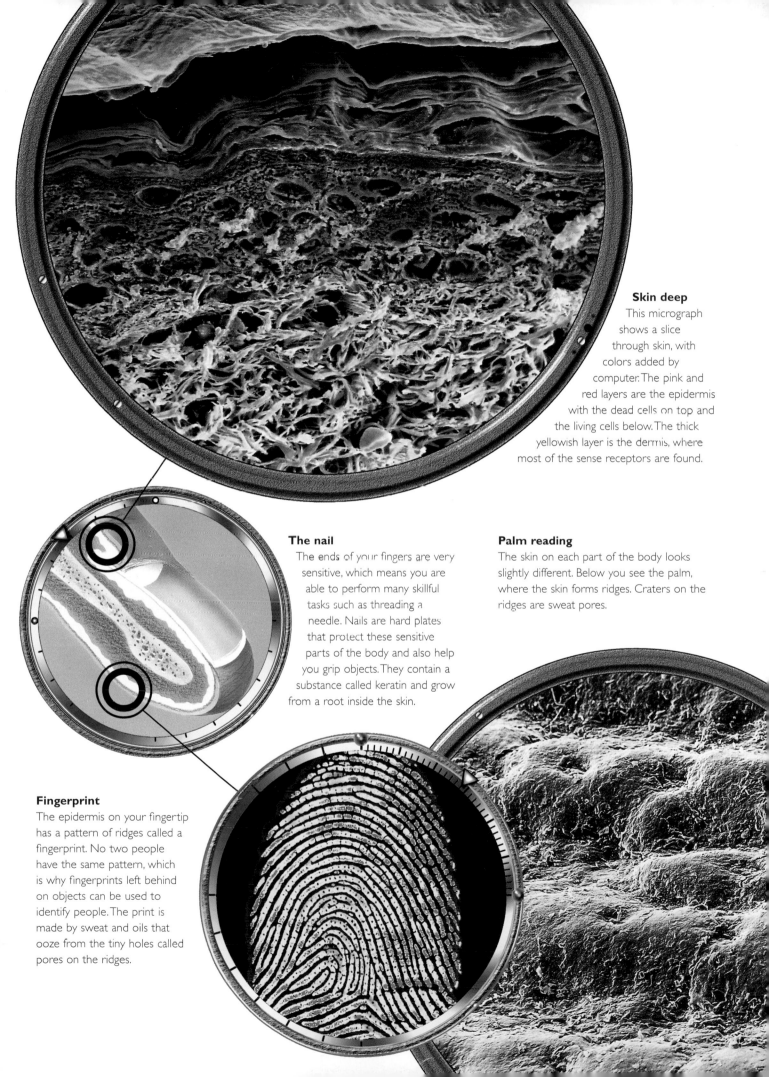

Skin deep

This micrograph shows a slice through skin, with colors added by computer. The pink and red layers are the epidermis with the dead cells on top and the living cells below. The thick yellowish layer is the dermis, where most of the sense receptors are found.

The nail

The ends of your fingers are very sensitive, which means you are able to perform many skillful tasks such as threading a needle. Nails are hard plates that protect these sensitive parts of the body and also help you grip objects. They contain a substance called keratin and grow from a root inside the skin.

Palm reading

The skin on each part of the body looks slightly different. Below you see the palm, where the skin forms ridges. Craters on the ridges are sweat pores.

Fingerprint

The epidermis on your fingertip has a pattern of ridges called a fingerprint. No two people have the same pattern, which is why fingerprints left behind on objects can be used to identify people. The print is made by sweat and oils that ooze from the tiny holes called pores on the ridges.

FEELING

Your sense of touch tells you a lot about an object. Pick up a few different things, and experience this for yourself. Feel each one, and describe it as fully as you can. Is it hard or soft, hot or cold, light or heavy, smooth or rough?

You are able to discover so much through touch because there are several types of sense receptor in the skin, and each one detects something different. Usually several receptors are stimulated at the same time. The receptors send signals to the brain, and the brain helps you build up a fuller picture of what you are touching.

People who are blind often develop a highly sensitive sense of touch. They learn to recognize people by feeling their faces and to read by feeling an alphabet of raised dots, a system known as braille.

Free nerve endings (detect pain, heat, cold)

Touch receptors

Epidermis

Dermis

Hair trigger
This micrograph shows hairs growing out of the skin. The hairs have sense receptors at their roots, so when something brushes against the hairs, you feel it.

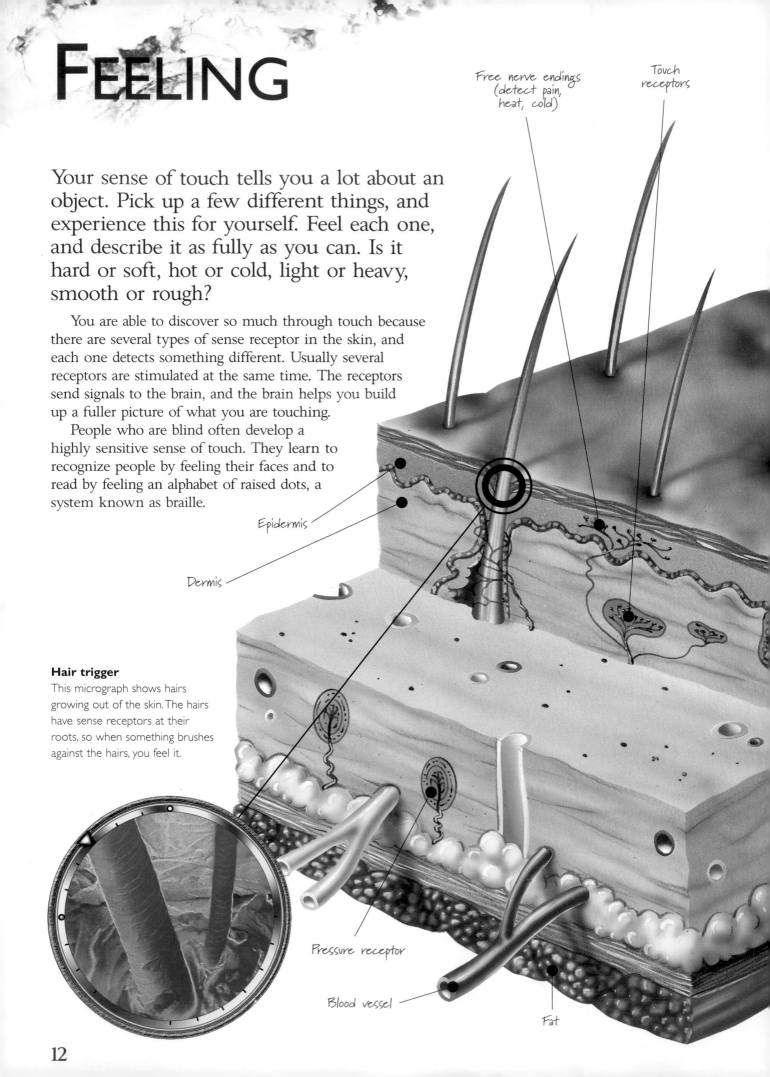

Pressure receptor

Blood vessel

Fat

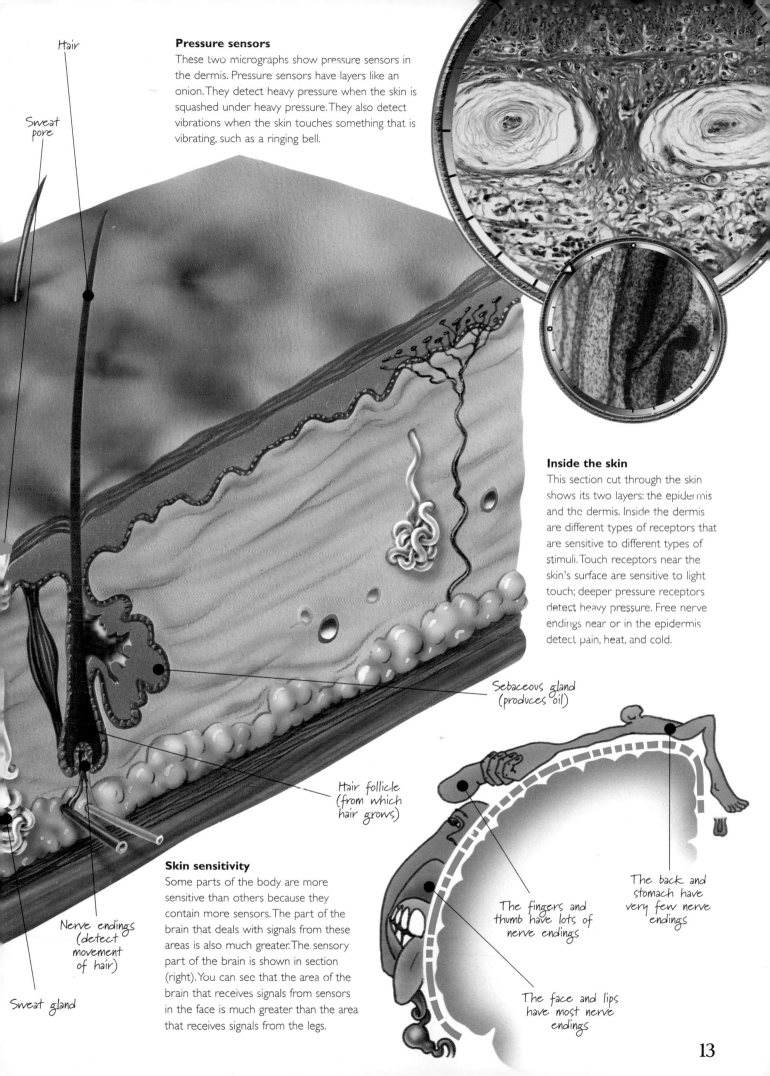

Pressure sensors
These two micrographs show pressure sensors in the dermis. Pressure sensors have layers like an onion. They detect heavy pressure when the skin is squashed under heavy pressure. They also detect vibrations when the skin touches something that is vibrating, such as a ringing bell.

Hair

Sweat pore

Inside the skin
This section cut through the skin shows its two layers: the epidermis and the dermis. Inside the dermis are different types of receptors that are sensitive to different types of stimuli. Touch receptors near the skin's surface are sensitive to light touch; deeper pressure receptors detect heavy pressure. Free nerve endings near or in the epidermis detect pain, heat, and cold.

Sebaceous gland (produces oil)

Hair follicle (from which hair grows)

Nerve endings (detect movement of hair)

Sweat gland

Skin sensitivity
Some parts of the body are more sensitive than others because they contain more sensors. The part of the brain that deals with signals from these areas is also much greater. The sensory part of the brain is shown in section (right). You can see that the area of the brain that receives signals from sensors in the face is much greater than the area that receives signals from the legs.

The fingers and thumb have lots of nerve endings

The back and stomach have very few nerve endings

The face and lips have most nerve endings

13

PROTECTING THE BODY

The world would be a very dangerous place if your sense of touch didn't help protect you. You feel your way down steps with your feet and your hand on the stair rail, for example, and you test that the water you wash with isn't too hot.

If you do hurt your body, you feel pain. This is a warning system that tells your brain something is happening that may harm your body, and you need to do something about it. There are two main types of pain – surface (superficial) pain and deep pain. You feel surface pain when you prick or cut yourself. The ache you feel when you sprain your ankle is a deep pain.

Signals from pain receptors travel along sensory neurons (nerve cells) inside nerves to the spinal cord. Here, association neurons relay nerve impulses to motor neurons. These carry messages to muscles that contract (pull) to move away the part of your body in danger. This is called a reflex action. A fraction of a second later, nerve impulses arrive in the brain (via the spinal cord) so that you can feel the pain.

Feeling hot
Sensors in the skin can tell you something is hot before you burn yourself by actually touching it.

Feeling cold
When cold receptors detect a chill, your brain interprets the message as the need to get warm.

Sudden pain
If you prick your finger, nerve signals travel to the spinal cord and back to the muscles so you can move away from danger. Signals also pass to the brain so that you feel the pain – but after you have moved your hand away.

Acid test
If acid drips on to your skin, it burns and stings, causing pain. You withdraw your hand quickly in a reflex action.

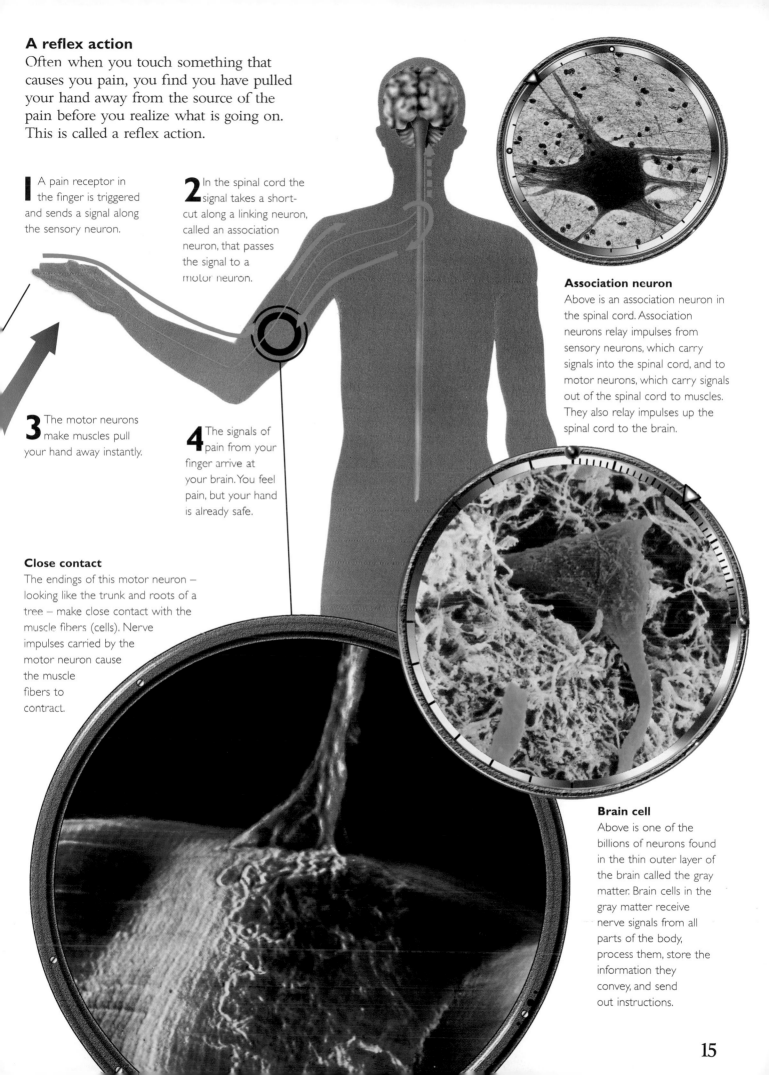

A reflex action

Often when you touch something that causes you pain, you find you have pulled your hand away from the source of the pain before you realize what is going on. This is called a reflex action.

1 A pain receptor in the finger is triggered and sends a signal along the sensory neuron.

2 In the spinal cord the signal takes a short-cut along a linking neuron, called an association neuron, that passes the signal to a motor neuron.

3 The motor neurons make muscles pull your hand away instantly.

4 The signals of pain from your finger arrive at your brain. You feel pain, but your hand is already safe.

Close contact

The endings of this motor neuron — looking like the trunk and roots of a tree — make close contact with the muscle fibers (cells). Nerve impulses carried by the motor neuron cause the muscle fibers to contract.

Association neuron

Above is an association neuron in the spinal cord. Association neurons relay impulses from sensory neurons, which carry signals into the spinal cord, and to motor neurons, which carry signals out of the spinal cord to muscles. They also relay impulses up the spinal cord to the brain.

Brain cell

Above is one of the billions of neurons found in the thin outer layer of the brain called the gray matter. Brain cells in the gray matter receive nerve signals from all parts of the body, process them, store the information they convey, and send out instructions.

BODY TEMPERATURE

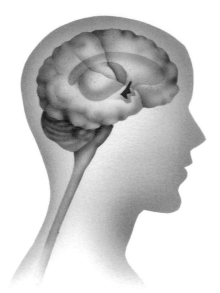

The cells in your body are constantly releasing heat that keeps you warm. Whatever the weather is like outside, the temperature of your body should always be 98.6°F (37°C). The temperature inside your body is monitored by a sensor in the brain called the hypothalamus. If you are too hot or too cold, the hypothalamus triggers processes in the skin that cool you down or warm you up.

The skin responds in several different ways. If your body temperature is too high, the skin releases sweat from sweat glands onto its surface. As the sweat evaporates, it drains heat from the body and cools you down. Blood vessels in the dermis get wider and act like radiators so that more heat is lost from blood. If your body temperature is too low, these blood vessels get narrower so that you lose less heat. In addition, you shiver — your body muscles contract and generate heat.

The hypothalamus

The hypothalamus controls several of the body's activities, including temperature control. If the temperature of the blood passing through the brain is too high or low, the hypothalamus sends signals to the skin to help bring the temperature back to normal.

Keeping cool

When your body gets hot, extra blood is carried to just below the surface of the skin so it can give off heat. This is why you flush when you are hot. Your skin also releases sweat to help you cool down, and the hairs on the skin flatten to allow cool air to reach the skin.

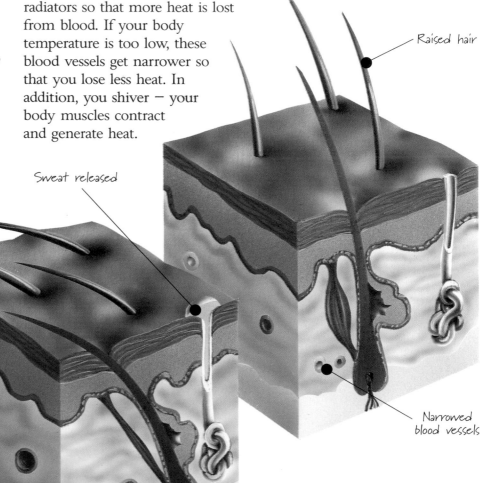

Raised hair

Sweat released

Flattened hairs

Wider blood vessels

Narrowed blood vessels

Keeping warm

When it is cold, blood vessels under the skin narrow to reduce heat loss, and hairs on the skin are pulled upright (giving you goose bumps) to trap a layer of warm air.

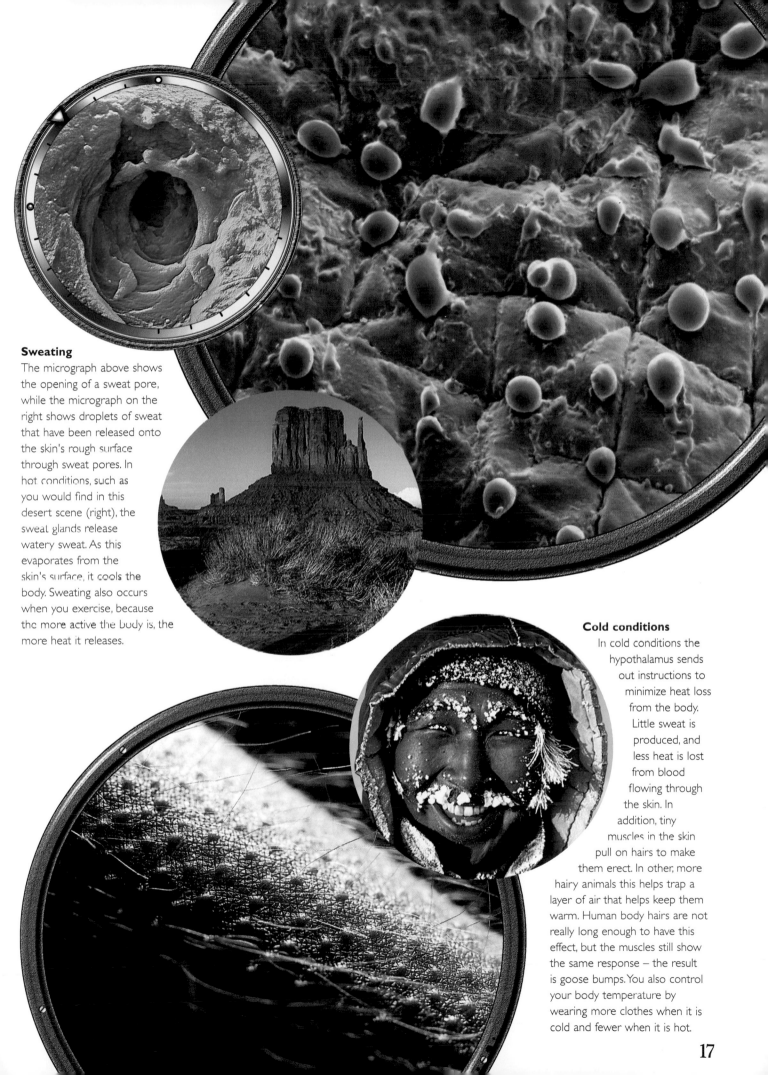

Sweating

The micrograph above shows the opening of a sweat pore, while the micrograph on the right shows droplets of sweat that have been released onto the skin's rough surface through sweat pores. In hot conditions, such as you would find in this desert scene (right), the sweat glands release watery sweat. As this evaporates from the skin's surface, it cools the body. Sweating also occurs when you exercise, because the more active the body is, the more heat it releases.

Cold conditions

In cold conditions the hypothalamus sends out instructions to minimize heat loss from the body. Little sweat is produced, and less heat is lost from blood flowing through the skin. In addition, tiny muscles in the skin pull on hairs to make them erect. In other, more hairy animals this helps trap a layer of air that helps keep them warm. Human body hairs are not really long enough to have this effect, but the muscles still show the same response – the result is goose bumps. You also control your body temperature by wearing more clothes when it is cold and fewer when it is hot.

17

TASTE

Find a mirror, poke out your tongue, and look closely at its surface. (Take a clean finger and feel the surface, too.) You will be able to see thousands of tiny bumps, called papillae. On the sides of the papillae are taste buds. These are so small you can see them only with a microscope, but they detect the taste of the food you eat.

As we chew our food, small particles of it dissolve into the saliva in our mouths. Once they are dissolved, substances in these particles can come into contact with the taste buds. The taste buds send information about the food to the brain.

Although there are many different substances in food, the tongue detects only four main tastes: sweet, sour, salt, and bitter. This is because most taste buds are more sensitive to one of these tastes than to any of the others. Groups of taste buds sensitive to one taste − sour, for example − are arranged together in certain parts of the tongue. Your sense of taste works together with your sense of smell to give you the flavor of the food you eat. The ability to smell and taste food gives you an appetite to eat good food and discourages you from eating bad or unsuitable food.

A taste map

Taste buds are sensitive to four basic tastes: sweet, sour, salt, and bitter. Certain parts of the tongue are more sensitive to one taste than to others.

A taste bud

In this micrograph you can see in blue the opening of a taste bud. Inside it you can see the hair tips of the 40 or so receptor cells that fit together like the segments of an orange. When food dissolved in saliva seeps in through the opening to the taste bud, it touches the hairs at the top of each receptor. These send signals along nerve fibers to the brain, which recognizes the taste.

The back of the tongue
Look in the mirror, and poke your tongue right out. You should be able to see the big round vallate papillae that form an upside-down V-shape at the back of the tongue. This is where bitter tastes are sensed.

The front of the tongue
At the tip of the tongue there is a mix of fungiform (mushroomlike) papillae and filiform (hairlike) papillae. Fungiform papillae carry taste buds that detect sweet, salt, and sour tastes. Filiform papillae do not have any taste buds.

Feeling flavor
The tongue does not just taste food, it also feels the food to tell you about its texture and temperature. All this information helps you recognize what you are eating. Texture and temperature are part of the fun of eating. An ice cream just wouldn't be the same if it wasn't smooth and cold.

A rough surface
In the micrograph above left you can see fungiform papillae from the tip of the tongue. Below you can see (in gold) the pointed tips of filiform papillae, which play no part in tasting. They give your tongue a rough surface so that you can grip food and move it around your mouth during chewing.

19

SMELL

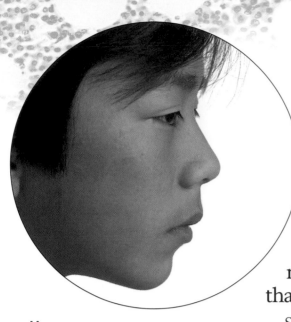

As soon as fresh bread is taken from the oven, you notice a delicious smell. This is because smelly substances from the bread mix with the air, and as you breathe, the air passes over smell receptors deep inside your nose. These receptors send signals to the brain that help you recognize the smell.

Up your nose

Air enters the nose through your nostrils when you breathe in and passes into the nasal cavity on its way to the lungs. Air carries tiny "smelly" particles or molecules. Some of these dissolve in the moist covering of the upper part of the nasal cavity. Here they are detected by smell receptors that send signals to the brain, where you sense the molecules as smells.

Scientists are still not sure exactly how different smells are detected, but our sense of smell is very sensitive. Smell is 20,000 times more sensitive than taste, and the human nose can identify around 10,000 different smells.

Your sense of smell works very closely with your sense of taste. Together they enable you to detect the flavor of food. Smell also helps you feel hungry – when you sniff something good – and puts you off eating something that is foul-smelling and bad. If your nose is blocked, with a cold for example, you can barely detect food flavor because you are depending solely on your less sensitive sense of taste.

The nose's other important job is to ensure that the air you breathe is clean and safe. Dust in the air is trapped by tiny hairs in the nose, and the air is warmed in the nose before it enters the lungs. On their way through the brain smell signals pass through an area that is responsible for memories and feelings. This may be the reason that smells bring back memories and can affect the way we feel. For example, wherever you might be, the smell of fresh bread might make you feel happy because it reminds you of home.

Air cleaners

This micrograph shows some of the hairlike cilia that line the nasal cavity. Cilia are covered with wet, sticky mucus. This traps any dust and dirt that enters the nose when you breathe in. The cilia beat rhythmically and move the mucus and trapped dust to the throat, where it is swallowed. By removing dust from breathed air, these cilia help protect the delicate tissues of the lungs from damage.

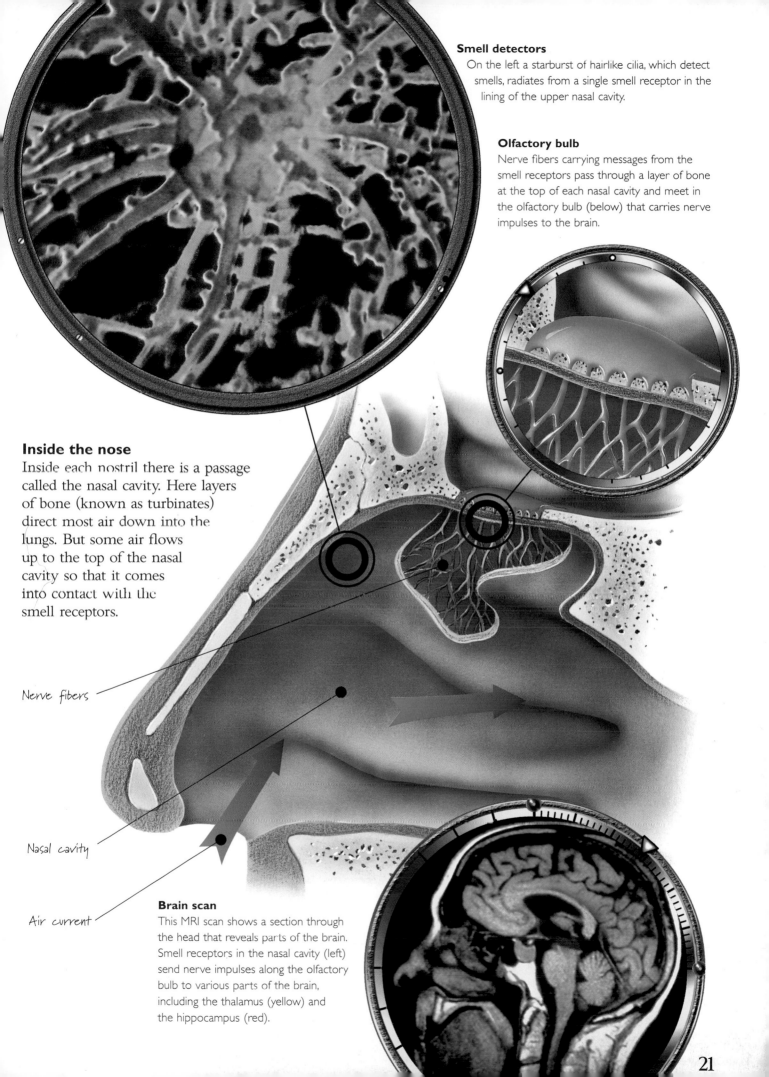

Smell detectors
On the left a starburst of hairlike cilia, which detect smells, radiates from a single smell receptor in the lining of the upper nasal cavity.

Olfactory bulb
Nerve fibers carrying messages from the smell receptors pass through a layer of bone at the top of each nasal cavity and meet in the olfactory bulb (below) that carries nerve impulses to the brain.

Inside the nose
Inside each nostril there is a passage called the nasal cavity. Here layers of bone (known as turbinates) direct most air down into the lungs. But some air flows up to the top of the nasal cavity so that it comes into contact with the smell receptors.

Nerve fibers

Nasal cavity

Air current

Brain scan
This MRI scan shows a section through the head that reveals parts of the brain. Smell receptors in the nasal cavity (left) send nerve impulses along the olfactory bulb to various parts of the brain, including the thalamus (yellow) and the hippocampus (red).

THE EAR

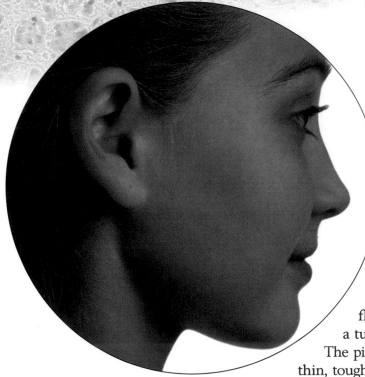

Your ears are very important sense organs because they help you both hear and balance. The ear flap that you see on the side of your head is just one part of the ear. The sense organs lie deep inside your skull.

The ear is divided into three parts — the outer ear, the middle ear, and the inner ear. The outer ear is the ear flap, called the pinna, on the side of your head as well as a tubelike passage leading into the head, called the ear canal. The pinna directs sounds into the ear canal and on toward a thin, tough membrane stretched right across it called the eardrum.

On the other side of the eardrum is the middle ear. Three tiny bones cross the middle ear and transmit sounds from the outer ear to the middle ear.

The inner ear contains the sense organs for hearing and balance. The organ that enables you to hear sounds is called the cochlea, and it looks like a snail shell. There are two sets of balance organs called the semicircular canals and the utricle and saccule.

Sound detectors

The delicate sense organs of the ear are invisible from the outside because they are surrounded and protected by the bones of the skull. The only visible part of the ear is the ear flap or pinna. The pinna is so shaped that it funnels sound waves into the ear canal that carries them inward to the sound detectors.

Protected by the skull
The sense organs of the ear fit neatly into a thick bony part of the skull.

Ear wax
The ear canal produces a sticky wax and is lined with small hairs. Both the hairs and the wax protect the eardrum by trapping any dust.

The pinna
The outer ear, which is also called the pinna, is made of a rubbery tissue called cartilage. No two people have pinnas that are exactly the same shape.

The organ of Corti
Deep inside your ear, within the cochlea, is the organ of Corti that converts sound vibrations into noise signals. In this micrograph you can see hair cells (yellow and pink) that turn sound waves into nerve impulses.

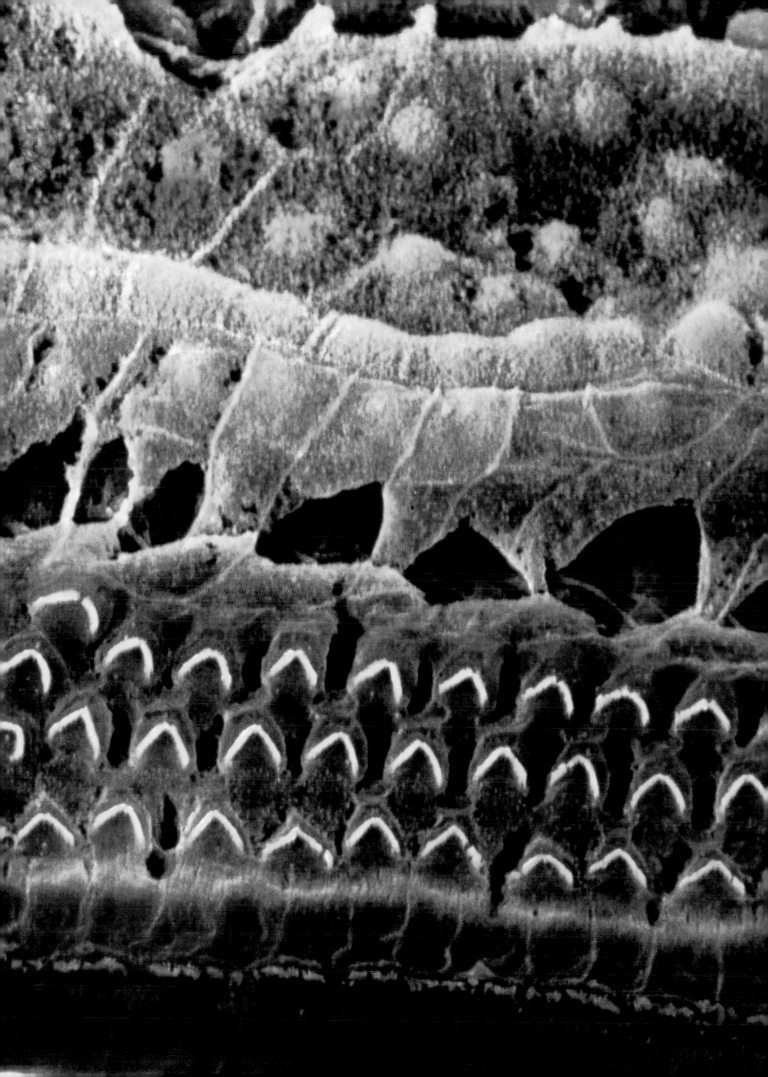

HEARING

Sound travels through the air in invisible waves. In order for you to hear these waves, they must be turned into sounds by your ears.

Sound waves are collected by the ear flap and channeled into the ear canal. Inside the ear canal they hit the tight membrane of the eardrum and are turned into vibrations. These vibrations knock the first of three tiny bones that are linked together in the middle ear. These are called the malleus (hammer), the incus (anvil), and the stapes (stirrup), and they are the smallest bones in the body. The malleus passes on vibrations to the incus and the incus to the stapes.

The stapes bone passes the vibrations into the inner ear through a membrane called the oval window. The outer and middle ear are filled with air, but the inner ear is filled with liquid. Vibrations passing through the window set up ripples in the liquid. These ripples bend hairlike receptor cells in the organ of Corti inside the cochlea — the "hearing" part of the ear. As the hairs bend, they produce nerve impulses that are carried by the auditory nerve to the brain, where they are interpreted as sounds.

Swapping sounds

Using a telephone is a true two-way process. Just like your ear, the mouthpiece of a telephone turns vibrations of sound into electrical impulses. The phone's earpiece turns electrical impulses into sound vibrations – that your ear turns into electrical impulses again!

Hearing hairs

This is a high magnification closeup of the the tiny hair cells inside the organ of Corti in your inner ear. These are the real sound receptors. They are washed over by a fluid called endolymph. As sound ripples through the endolymph, so the endolymph wafts the hairs to and fro, triggering them into sending sound signals to your brain.

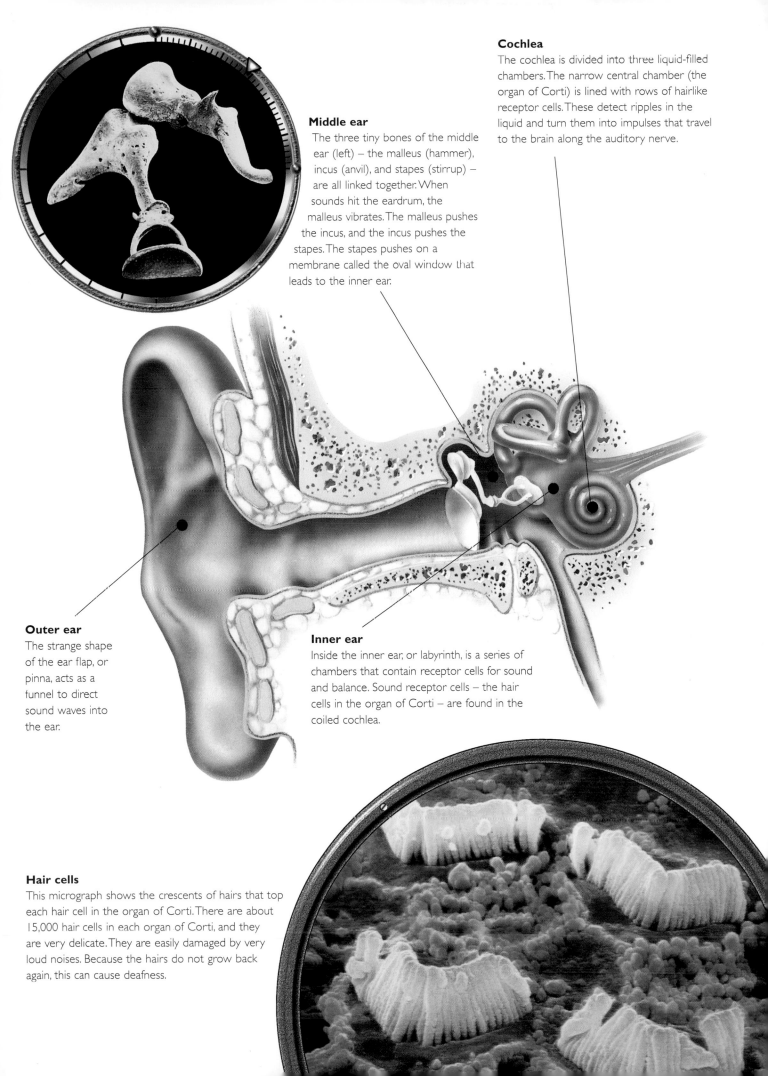

Cochlea

The cochlea is divided into three liquid-filled chambers. The narrow central chamber (the organ of Corti) is lined with rows of hairlike receptor cells. These detect ripples in the liquid and turn them into impulses that travel to the brain along the auditory nerve.

Middle ear

The three tiny bones of the middle ear (left) – the malleus (hammer), incus (anvil), and stapes (stirrup) – are all linked together. When sounds hit the eardrum, the malleus vibrates. The malleus pushes the incus, and the incus pushes the stapes. The stapes pushes on a membrane called the oval window that leads to the inner ear.

Outer ear

The strange shape of the ear flap, or pinna, acts as a funnel to direct sound waves into the ear.

Inner ear

Inside the inner ear, or labyrinth, is a series of chambers that contain receptor cells for sound and balance. Sound receptor cells – the hair cells in the organ of Corti – are found in the coiled cochlea.

Hair cells

This micrograph shows the crescents of hairs that top each hair cell in the organ of Corti. There are about 15,000 hair cells in each organ of Corti, and they are very delicate. They are easily damaged by very loud noises. Because the hairs do not grow back again, this can cause deafness.

DISTINGUISHING SOUNDS

The rush of water
Sound is only vibrations in the air – yet we can pick up such subtle differences in the vibration pattern that we have no problem identifying thousands of different sounds.

When you throw a stone into a pond, ripples move outward, away from the disturbance. Sound waves disturb the air in a similar way.

Different sounds make different waves, from gentle ripples to strong waves that your whole body can feel. But it is only when these sound waves reach the delicate parts of your inner ear that you can actually hear them. Having two ears helps you work out exactly where a sound is coming from. If you are right in front of a sound, it will reach both ears at the same time. If the sound is to one side of you, the ear nearest to the sound will hear it less than one-thousandth of a second earlier than the other ear, and slightly louder. The brain notices this difference and may automatically turn your head toward the sound.

Sound waves
The shape of a sound wave depends on the sound that is made. The height of a wave tells you about the volume of a sound. Loud sounds, like those produced by a jet airplane taking off, produce very tall waves. The distance between the highs and lows of the wave, called the wavelength or frequency, tells you about the pitch of a sound. A violin can produce very high-pitched sounds when its vibrating strings generate a lot of short waves in succession.

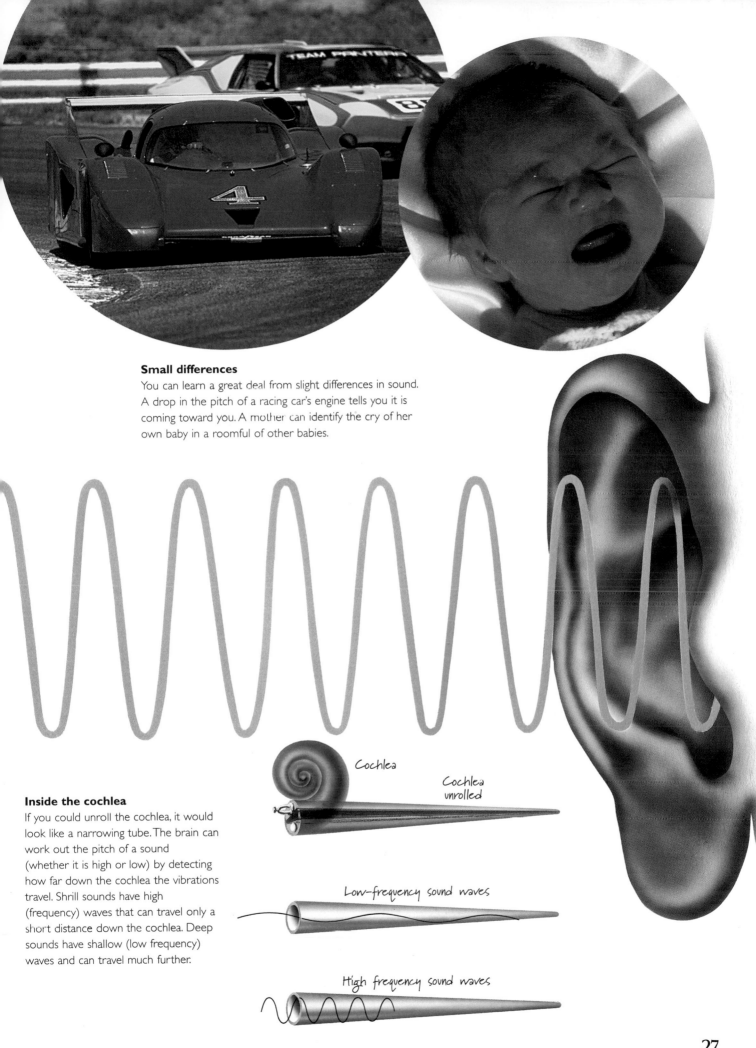

Small differences

You can learn a great deal from slight differences in sound. A drop in the pitch of a racing car's engine tells you it is coming toward you. A mother can identify the cry of her own baby in a roomful of other babies.

Inside the cochlea

If you could unroll the cochlea, it would look like a narrowing tube. The brain can work out the pitch of a sound (whether it is high or low) by detecting how far down the cochlea the vibrations travel. Shrill sounds have high (frequency) waves that can travel only a short distance down the cochlea. Deep sounds have shallow (low frequency) waves and can travel much further.

Cochlea

Cochlea unrolled

Low-frequency sound waves

High frequency sound waves

BALANCE ON THE MOVE

Balancing act
Walking on stilts calls for a very good sense of balance, for a stiltwalker is very top-heavy. This girl can stay up on stilts because the balance organs in her ears tell her constantly when she is near toppling. Every time she moves, the changes in position registered by the balance organs are fed back to her brain. Her brain works out what adjustments she needs to make, often without her even thinking about it, and sends out the right commands to her body.

Moving your head
Your brain knows whether your head is moving from side to side, or backward and forward, because different movements make the hair receptor cells in your inner ear move in different ways, too, and send different signals. When the head moves quickly, it sends more signals than when it moves slowly.

If you have ever played with a jointed doll and tried to make it do everyday movements, such as walk, sit down, or stand up, you will know that it is surprisingly complicated.

To get the doll to stand up by itself, for example, you need to play around with the position of the body, legs, arms, and head for quite a while until you can make the doll balance.

Luckily for you, your brain is constantly correcting the position of your body so that you don't fall over. It can do this because it is sent information from sensors all over your body, but the body's main balancing organs are in your ears. The organ of balance is called the vestibular apparatus. It has two systems, which work together. One system helps you balance as you move. It is made up of three tiny arched tubes, called semicircular canals. The other system tells you what position your head is in and in which direction you are moving. This system is found in two bulges near the base of the semicircular canals, called the utricle and saccule.

The semicircular canals

Deep inside the inner ear are three arched tubes filled with liquid. These are called the semicircular canals. As you move your head, the liquid in the three tubes moves. At one end of each tube there is a swelling called the ampulla. The ampulla contains the cupula, which detects the movement of the liquid.

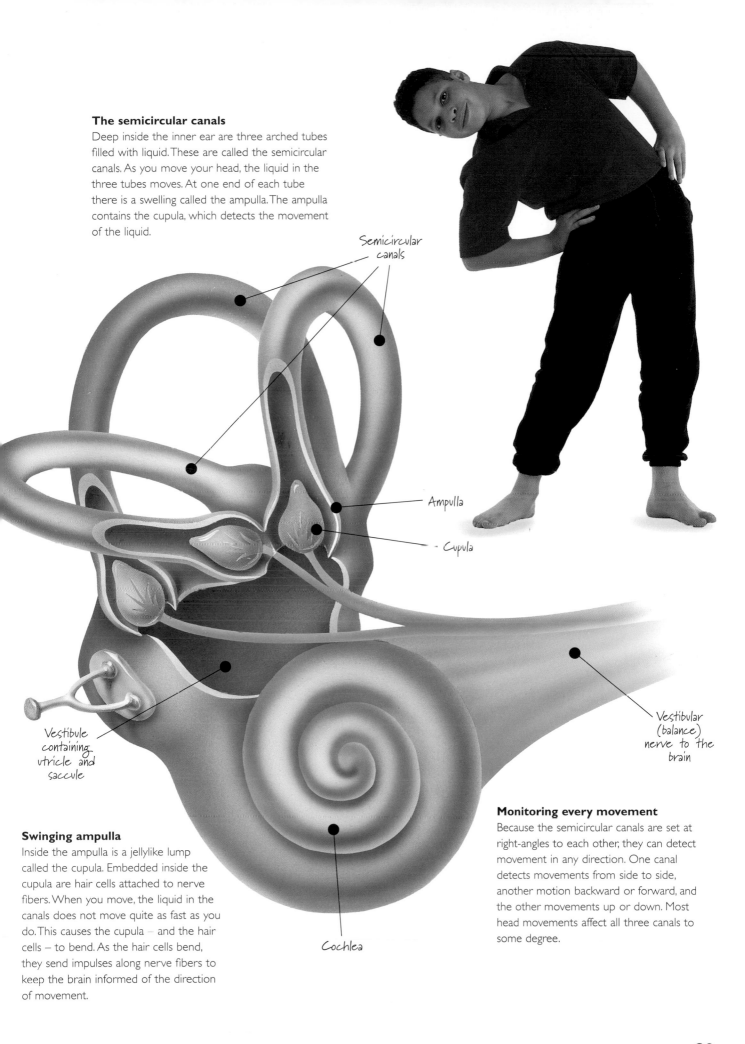

Semicircular canals

Ampulla

Cupula

Vestibule containing utricle and saccule

Vestibular (balance) nerve to the brain

Cochlea

Swinging ampulla

Inside the ampulla is a jellylike lump called the cupula. Embedded inside the cupula are hair cells attached to nerve fibers. When you move, the liquid in the canals does not move quite as fast as you do. This causes the cupula – and the hair cells – to bend. As the hair cells bend, they send impulses along nerve fibers to keep the brain informed of the direction of movement.

Monitoring every movement

Because the semicircular canals are set at right-angles to each other, they can detect movement in any direction. One canal detects movements from side to side, another motion backward or forward, and the other movements up or down. Most head movements affect all three canals to some degree.

29

WHICH WAY UP?

Inside the inner ear — in the vestibule that lies between the semicircular canals and the cochlea — are two sensory structures that tell you which way up you are. These are the utricle and saccule, and they are sensitive to gravity. Gravity is the invisible force that pulls us down toward the Earth.

Because the body's balancing system relies on gravity, it does not work in space, where there is no gravity. When astronauts living in a space station go to bed, they do not lie down because there is no up or down. To sleep, they strap themselves into their sleeping bags, which might run any way along one of the walls (there is no floor or ceiling — all the surfaces are walls). But they never feel that they are the wrong way up because there is no right way up for their balance systems to detect.

Though the main organs of balance are in the inner ear, your body also uses other information to help it balance. There are sensors in your muscles, tendons, and skin. Your eyes, too, help the body judge its position, work out how fast it can move, and how to avoid colliding with other objects.

Spaced out

One of the problems astronauts have to cope with is space sickness. Without gravity the balance sensors all over the body do not behave in the usual way and send confusing messages to the brain. This leaves astronauts feeling sick and dizzy. It's rather like the dizzying confusion of signals you get when you spin around and around too fast.

On your head

This woman can carry a heavy load on her head because her utricles and saccules constantly monitor the position of her head and enable her brain to send messages to neck muscles that keep the head upright.

The macula

Inside both the utricle and saccule is an area called the macula (right). Here there are rows of receptors with hairlike cells sticking out of them (shown in purple). These hair cells point into a layer of jelly (yellow), and the jelly is covered with a layer of microscopic stones, called otoliths (red). Otoliths respond to the pull of gravity by pulling the hair cells and making them bend. The amount of "pull" depends on whether you are upright or upside-down. When stimulated, hair cells send impulses to the brain. The brain works out your position by interpreting the numbers and patterns of impulses arriving from the hair cells.

THE EYE

Sight is the sense we rely on above all others. More of the brain is dedicated to vision than to any other sense, and four-fifths of all the information received by the brain comes from the eyes.

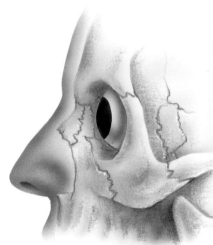

The eye responds to light. We see the things around us because they give off reflected light from the Sun and other light sources, and the eye turns this light into nerve impulses. The impulses are then turned into the pictures we see by a part of the brain called the visual cortex.

The brain makes sense of what it is seeing by looking for patterns and comparing them with other patterns it is familiar with. Incredibly, this process of "seeing" happens instantly. As soon as you see something, you recognize it, and this process carries on as long as you are awake.

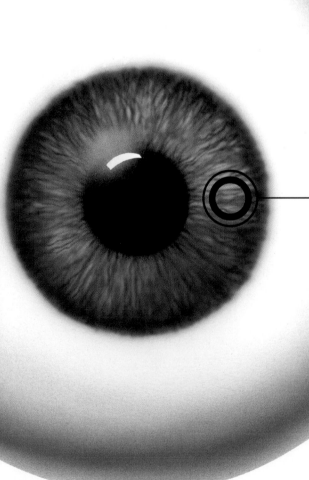

The window of the eye

The transparent tissue at the front of the eye is called the cornea. Behind the cornea is a circle of muscles called the iris. These muscles adjust the size of the pupil to control how much light passes through to the sensitive parts of the eye.

The eye socket

The eyeball sits in a hollow in the skull called an orbit or eye socket. It is cushioned by pads of fat and covered with slippery mucus, so that it can move around smoothly.

Eye color

The iris can be many different colors – blue, green, gray, or brown. In the micrograph above you can see the color cells (blue and brown) on the surface of the iris. Color depends on the amount of a substance called melanin in the iris. Brown eyes contain a lot of melanin, while blue eyes have little melanin and are more sensitive to light.

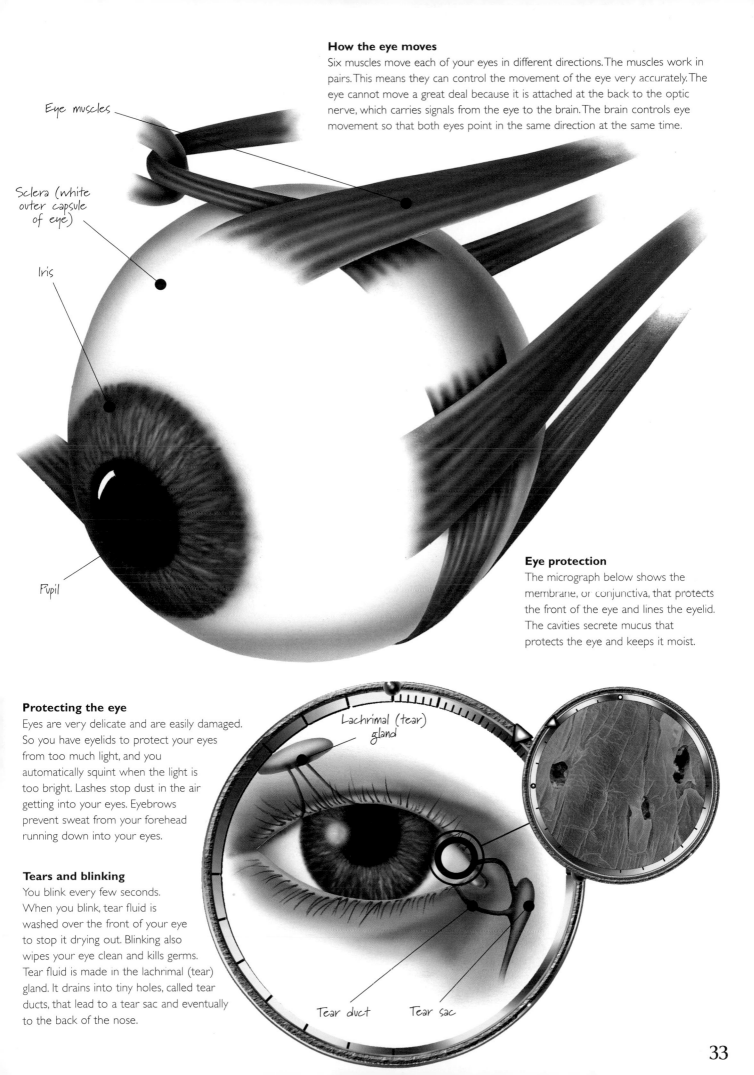

How the eye moves

Six muscles move each of your eyes in different directions. The muscles work in pairs. This means they can control the movement of the eye very accurately. The eye cannot move a great deal because it is attached at the back to the optic nerve, which carries signals from the eye to the brain. The brain controls eye movement so that both eyes point in the same direction at the same time.

Eye muscles

Sclera (white outer capsule of eye)

Iris

Pupil

Eye protection

The micrograph below shows the membrane, or conjunctiva, that protects the front of the eye and lines the eyelid. The cavities secrete mucus that protects the eye and keeps it moist.

Protecting the eye

Eyes are very delicate and are easily damaged. So you have eyelids to protect your eyes from too much light, and you automatically squint when the light is too bright. Lashes stop dust in the air getting into your eyes. Eyebrows prevent sweat from your forehead running down into your eyes.

Tears and blinking

You blink every few seconds. When you blink, tear fluid is washed over the front of your eye to stop it drying out. Blinking also wipes your eye clean and kills germs. Tear fluid is made in the lachrimal (tear) gland. It drains into tiny holes, called tear ducts, that lead to a tear sac and eventually to the back of the nose.

Lachrimal (tear) gland

Tear duct

Tear sac

FOCUSING LIGHT

Wide-eyed
In dim light the muscles of the iris relax to dilate (enlarge) the pupil and make it up to 16 times its smallest size to let in as much light as possible.

During every waking hour you look at objects that are close to your eyes — this book, for example — or far away — a house in the distance. Your eyes can detect objects clearly, whether they are far or near. Focusing happens automatically — without your thinking about it.

When you look at something, both eyes concentrate on it. The object may be close or far, but to see it clearly the eyes have to adjust so that the image of it falls exactly on the surface at the back of the eye called the retina. As light rays enter the eye, they are bent toward the pupil by the rounded surface of the cornea. The lens flattens or bulges to focus the image on the retina. Muscles around the lens — under the control of the brain — automatically adjust its shape so that the image on the retina is clear. On the retina are millions of receptor cells. If these cells are stimulated by light, they send impulses to the brain. The image that falls on the retina is inverted (upside-down). When the brain interprets the image, it also turns it the right way up.

Bright-eyed
In bright light the iris pulls the pupil inward to let in as little light as possible — to protect the eye and give a sharp image.

Inside the eye
Between the front of the eye and the iris is an area called the front chamber. It is filled with a transparent fluid called aqueous humor. Between the lens and the retina is the back chamber. Here there is a thicker fluid called the vitreous humor. Both humors support the eye and maintain its shape.

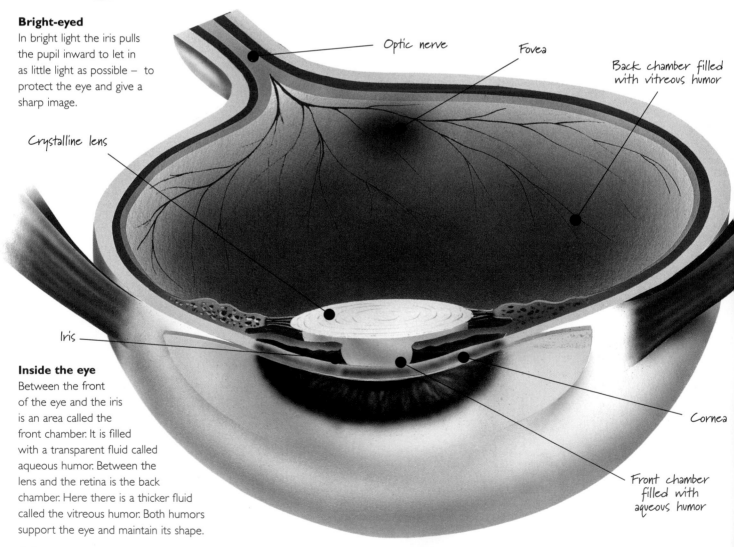

Optic nerve

Fovea

Back chamber filled with vitreous humor

Crystalline lens

Iris

Cornea

Front chamber filled with aqueous humor

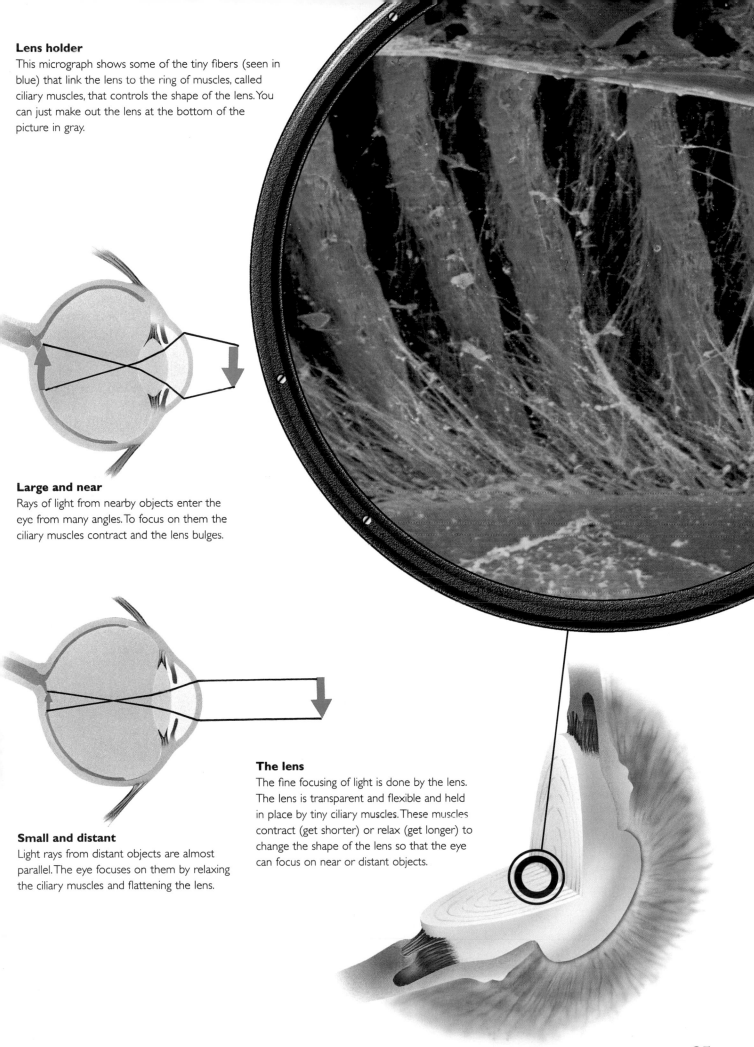

Lens holder

This micrograph shows some of the tiny fibers (seen in blue) that link the lens to the ring of muscles, called ciliary muscles, that controls the shape of the lens. You can just make out the lens at the bottom of the picture in gray.

Large and near

Rays of light from nearby objects enter the eye from many angles. To focus on them the ciliary muscles contract and the lens bulges.

Small and distant

Light rays from distant objects are almost parallel. The eye focuses on them by relaxing the ciliary muscles and flattening the lens.

The lens

The fine focusing of light is done by the lens. The lens is transparent and flexible and held in place by tiny ciliary muscles. These muscles contract (get shorter) or relax (get longer) to change the shape of the lens so that the eye can focus on near or distant objects.

HOW THE EYE WORKS

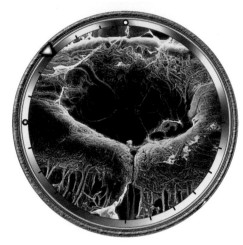

Vision center
The circular hollow in this micrograph is the fovea, the small area in the center of the retina where images are seen in greatest detail. Millions of nerves and blood vessels run in and out of it.

The cornea and lens of the eye focus light onto a layer called the retina that covers the inside of the back of the eye. The retina is light-sensitive because it is packed with receptor cells that fire off impulses to the brain when light hits them.

The retina contains over 130 million receptor cells called rods and cones. There are around 125 million rods and over 6 million cones. Rods help you see in dim light. Cones help you see in bright light and in color. Your eye focuses the object at the center of your gaze on the center of the retina. This area is called the fovea. The fovea is packed with cones. The brain uses signals sent by these cones to form the clearest and most detailed images. You can test this by looking at these words. Stare at two of the letters – you will see them clearly; letters on either side of them will not be so clear. Most of the cells in the rest of the retina are rods.

Seeing in color
There are three kinds of cone cell. Each is most sensitive to either blue, green, or red light. Together, all three enable you to see the full range of colors. Cones work only in bright light, but they react four times faster than rods and "see" in great detail as well as in color.

Shades of gray
Rods help you see in dim light, but they are able to make pictures only in black and white. Rods are found mostly around the sides of the retina. They make it possible for you to see things around the object you are focusing on.

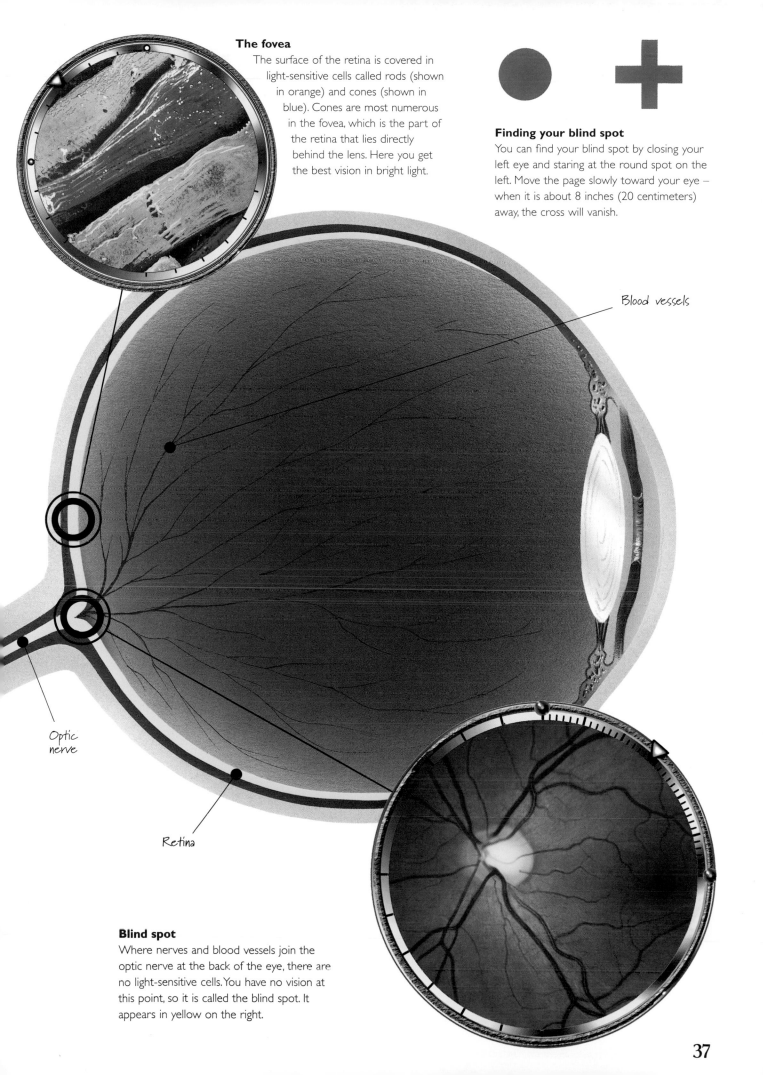

The fovea

The surface of the retina is covered in light-sensitive cells called rods (shown in orange) and cones (shown in blue). Cones are most numerous in the fovea, which is the part of the retina that lies directly behind the lens. Here you get the best vision in bright light.

Finding your blind spot

You can find your blind spot by closing your left eye and staring at the round spot on the left. Move the page slowly toward your eye — when it is about 8 inches (20 centimeters) away, the cross will vanish.

Blood vessels

Optic nerve

Retina

Blind spot

Where nerves and blood vessels join the optic nerve at the back of the eye, there are no light-sensitive cells. You have no vision at this point, so it is called the blind spot. It appears in yellow on the right.

VISUAL PATHWAYS

You do not actually "see" something until the impulses from the rods and cones in the retina have traveled down the optic nerves to an area at the back of the brain called the visual cortex.

Here the impulses are sorted out and interpreted. Some information may be sent on to specialized areas of the brain that deal with color or movement.

On their journey to the brain the impulses from each eye do not travel separately. In the center of the brain the optic nerves meet at a crossroads called the optic chiasma. Here some nerve fibers split off. All the impulses from the right side of each eye travel together to the right side of the brain. Impulses from the left side of each eye travel to the left side of the brain. This enables the brain to compare information from both eyes so that it can form images with depth and judge distance effectively.

Stereo vision
Each eye has a slightly different view of the outside world. The brain merges impulses received from each eye to produce a single image that has depth.

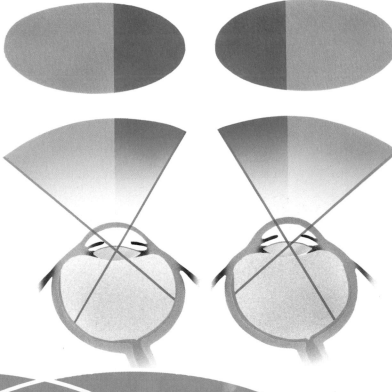

Two views
These pictures show the different views from the left eye and right eye. The brain joins these pictures together to give one wide picture.

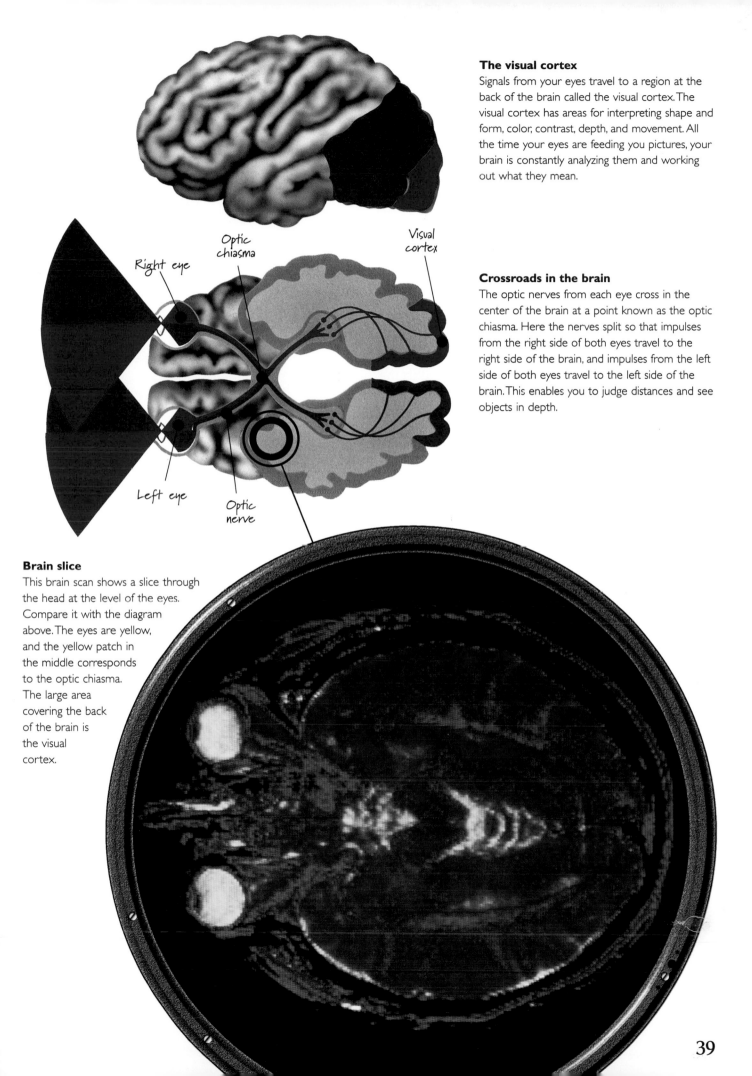

The visual cortex

Signals from your eyes travel to a region at the back of the brain called the visual cortex. The visual cortex has areas for interpreting shape and form, color, contrast, depth, and movement. All the time your eyes are feeding you pictures, your brain is constantly analyzing them and working out what they mean.

Crossroads in the brain

The optic nerves from each eye cross in the center of the brain at a point known as the optic chiasma. Here the nerves split so that impulses from the right side of both eyes travel to the right side of the brain, and impulses from the left side of both eyes travel to the left side of the brain. This enables you to judge distances and see objects in depth.

Optic chiasma

Visual cortex

Right eye

Left eye

Optic nerve

Brain slice

This brain scan shows a slice through the head at the level of the eyes. Compare it with the diagram above. The eyes are yellow, and the yellow patch in the middle corresponds to the optic chiasma. The large area covering the back of the brain is the visual cortex.

39

HOW WE SEE

Scientists are still not sure exactly how the brain makes sense of the information from the eyes. They believe that the brain builds up a store of memories and experiences and compares every image with what it already knows from this.

For example, you know from experience what size people usually are and what size trains usually are. But if you looked at a picture of a grown man next to a child's toy railway engine that was otherwise identical to the full-size engine, you might be confused for a moment. To work out if the man was a giant or the engine was small, you would look for other clues, comparing both objects with the size of a nearby tree.

Each time it looks at an object, the brain makes comparisons like this to discover more information, such as how far away the object is, how deep it is, what color it is, whether it is moving, and if it is flat or three-dimensional.

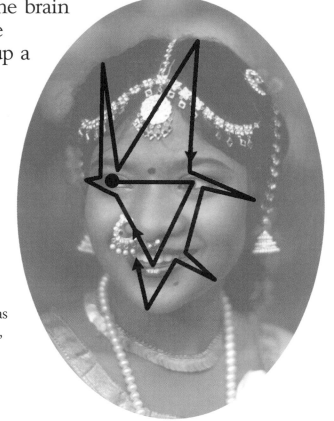

The restless eye
Your eyes are always moving. Even when you stare straight at someone, your eyes are darting around their face gathering information. This also helps the brain fill in any gaps caused by the blind spot. The lines on the face above trace the eye movement of someone looking at the picture for a couple of seconds.

Tricking your eyes
Your brain is not always sure what to make of what it is seeing. You can "see" this picture in different ways. Sometimes the front of the cube appears to stick out, but it can also look as if the front section is missing. Pictures like this are called optical illusions because they are made to trick the brain.

Joining up the dots

The color pictures you see in this book, like those in every other printed book or newspaper, are made up of tiny dots, as the enlargement of this photograph shows. The dots are so small that the brain simply joins them together into smooth color. TV pictures are made up of tiny dots in just the same way.

VISION PROBLEMS

Not all of us have perfect sight. The most common problems are difficulties in focusing, known as farsightedness and nearsightedness. These vision problems can be corrected with glasses or contact lenses.

You can have trouble focusing if your eyeball is not the right shape. Sometimes the front of the eye or the lens may not be the right shape. As people grow older, they often find it becomes difficult to see closeup work. This is usually because the lens has become less flexible.

It is important to have your eyes checked at least every two years. This will help detect sight problems early on. If your eyes have to work hard to correct vision problems, you may suffer from eyestrain and headaches. Eye checks are also important because they can reveal eye diseases and some diseases in other parts of the body.

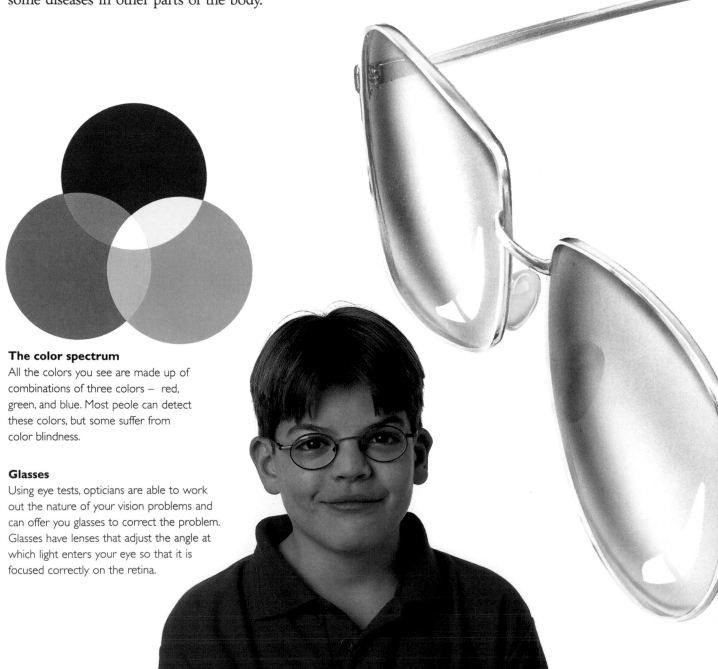

The color spectrum
All the colors you see are made up of combinations of three colors – red, green, and blue. Most peole can detect these colors, but some suffer from color blindness.

Glasses
Using eye tests, opticians are able to work out the nature of your vision problems and can offer you glasses to correct the problem. Glasses have lenses that adjust the angle at which light enters your eye so that it is focused correctly on the retina.

Nearsightedness

People who are nearsighted see close objects clearly, but distant objects focus just in front of the retina. This may be because the eyeball is too long, or the cornea too rounded.

Image focused in front of the retina

Farsightedness

People who are farsighted see distant objects clearly, while close objects are blurred because they focus just behind the retina. This may be because the eyeball is too small or too short, or the lens is too flat.

Image focused behind the retina

Color blindness

Different cones are sensitive to different colors. Some people do not see color in the same way as most people. This is because one or more of their groups of cones are missing or do not work properly. They may confuse the colors red and green or see things only in black and white and green. This is called color blindness and is mainly a male problem. It is often passed down through families. If you can see the number 29 in this picture, you have normal vision. If you can't see the number, you may have a problem with color vision.

43

ANIMAL VISION

You may think that you can see everything there is to see in the world around you, but there are animals that can see more than you can. These animals need especially good eyesight to be able to find food.

Cats, for example, have eyes that can see well in dim light so they can hunt for food at dawn and dusk. Birds of prey, like eagles, have eyes that can see clearly over long distances so they can look out for food from high up in the sky where they cannot be seen.

Some animals can see light that human eyes cannot detect. When you look at a leaf, what you actually see is the light reflected off the leaf. This light travels in waves, and every color has a different wavelength. Human eyes can see a range of colored light from violet, blue, green, yellow, and orange through to red. But there are colors of light just outside this range of wavelengths that animals such as insects are able to see. These are called ultraviolet light and infra-red light.

Ultraviolet patterns
Some flowers have patterns that can be seen only by insects and show them where the sweet nectar is. Insects can see these patterns because they are sensitive to ultraviolet light and human beings are not.

Night vision
In dim light a cat can see more than you can because the pupils of its eyes can open very wide to let in as much light as possible. Mirrorlike cells behind the retina also help by reflecting light back into the eye. This is why you can see a cat's eyes flashing in the dark.

Seeing infrared
Things that are hot give off infrared light. In a desert at night the human eye sees just blackness, but a rattlesnake can see the infrared light from objects that are warmer than the air, like the body of a live rat, its prey.

Eagle-eyed
You could probably see a rabbit 0.6 mile (1 kilometer) away, but an eagle can spot a rabbit 3 miles (5 kilometers) away. This is because it has five times as many rods and cones on the retina of its eyes as you do, so it can build up a much more detailed picture of what it is seeing.

Bee's-eye view
Bees and other insects have compound eyes. These are made up of many separate compartments, each with a lens. The insect's brain combines all the information from these compartments to form the type of image shown here. Many insects cannot see objects in detail but are very good at detecting sudden movements.

GLOSSARY

ASSOCIATION NEURON (Noo-ron)
Neuron that relays impulses from sensory neurons to motor neurons.

CELL
Cells are the building blocks of all living things. Very simple living things are made up of just a few cells, but your body is made up of billions of different types of cells.

CILIA (Sill-ee-uh)
Tiny hairlike structures attached to cells in certain parts of the body.

COCHLEA (Cock-lee-uh)
The coiled tube in the inner ear that looks like a snail shell. In the cochlea sounds are turned into signals that are sent to the brain so that we can hear them.

CORNEA (Core-nee-uh)
The transparent layer at the front of the eye that helps focus rays of light.

DERMIS (Durr-miss)
The inner layer of skin where touch sensors are found.

EARDRUM
A thin membrane/skin that separates the outer ear from the inner ear. The eardrum vibrates when sound waves hit it.

EPIDERMIS (Epee-durr-miss)
The outer layer of skin. It protects the living cells in the dermis.

GLAND
A part of the body that secretes a body chemical or liquid like sweat.

IRIS
The colored part of the eye – usually brown, blue, green, or gray. The size of the iris changes to control the amount of light that enters the eye.

KERATIN
The substance that hair, nails, and the outer layers of the skin are made of.

LENS
A transparent part of the eye. Its shape is changed to focus light on the back of the eye.

MOTOR NEURON (Noo-ron)
Neuron that carries nerve impulses from the brain and spinal cord to muscles.

MUCUS (Mew-kuss)
A thick, slippery substance that protects and moistens delicate parts of the body, like the inside of the nose.

MUSCLE
A body tissue that is able to get shorter and move parts of the body. Groups of muscles work together so that we are able to move our bodies.

NERVE
A bundle of neurons that relays nerve impulses between the brain and spinal cord and the body. Nerves carry nerve impulses from the sense organs to the brain.

NEURON (Noo-ron)
A nerve cell that transmits electrical signals. Bundles of neurons make up nerves.

PORE
A tiny opening.

PUPIL
The dark middle part of the eye. The pupil is in fact an opening in the iris that changes size to let in as much or as little light as you need to see.

RECEPTOR CELL
Cell that responds to some form of stimulation. Receptor cells in the eye respond to light, those in the ear to sound. Receptor cells in the nose and mouth respond to substances in food or in the air. Skin receptors respond to many different things, including pressure, pain, and temperature.

RETINA
The light-sensitive layer at the back of the eye.

RODS AND CONES
The tiny cells on the surface of the retina that are sensitive to light and that send signals to the brain.

SALIVA
The watery substance in your mouth that helps you taste, chew, and digest food.

SEMICIRCULAR CANALS
(Sem-ee-sir-kyuh-lur)
Three tiny arches in the inner ear that are filled with liquid. They send your brain information about your body's movements to help you balance.

SENSORY NEURON (Noo-ron)
Neuron that carries nerve impulses from sensory receptors to the brain and spinal cord.

SPINAL CORD (Spy-nall)
The column of nervous tissue that passes through your backbone and links the brain to the nerves.

TASTE BUD
A bunch of receptor cells found mainly on the tongue. They detect substances in food and drink.

UTRICLE AND SACCULE
(Yoo-trick-ull and Sack-yool)
Tiny balance organs in your inner ear that give your brain information about the position of the head and the direction you are moving in.

VESTIBULAR APPARATUS
(Vess-tib-yuh-lur)
The name for all of your body's balance organs. These are the semicircular canals and the utricle and saccule.

SET INDEX

Volume numbers are in **bold**, followed by page numbers.

A adrenal glands **8:** 40-41, 44, 46

alveoli (air sacs) **5:** 10-11, 19, 22-23, 34, 36-37, 38, 46

ankle **2:** 9, 28-29, 34, **7:** 12, 32

aorta **1:** 9, 12, 14-15, 16, 46

arm **2:** 10, 24-25, 31; muscles **7:** 8-9, 11, 12-13, 15, 16, 22-23, 30-31

arteries **1:** 8-9, 10-11, 18, 46, **3:** 25, 41, **5:** 46; coronary **1:** 18-19, 44, 46; disease **1:** 44-45; pulmonary **1:** 14, **5:** 18-19, 23

autonomic nervous system **7:** 38, 40, **8:** 8, 33, 38-39, 46

axon **6:** 9, **8:** 10, 14-15, 17, 24-25, 46

B babies **3:** 43, **5:** 24, **4:** 6-7, 8, 28-29, 30, 38; skeleton **2:** 4, 14-15, 16, 20, 46

backbone see spine

balance **6:** 22, 28-29, 30, 46; **8:** 4, 20-21, 34-35, 46

biceps muscle **2:** 25, 34, **7:** 9, 13, 16, 22-23, 24-25

birth **4:** 25, 28-29, **5:** 24, **7:** 39, **8:** 40

bladder **3:** 38-39, 40-41, 42-43, 46

blood **1:** 6, 10, 20-21, 22-23; breathing **5:** 10, 18, 22, 29, 42, 46; clotting **1:** 21, 26, 28-29, 44-45, 46; muscles **7:** 6, 18, 40-41; nutrients **3:** 8-9, 10-11, 22, 24-25, 31, 46; reproduction **4:** 10-11, 12; water **3:** 36, 38-39, 40-41

blood cells **1:** 20-21, 46; manufacture **1:** 30-31, **2:** 6, 12-13; red **1:** 6, 8, 20 21, 22, 24-25, 46, **3:** 24, 33, **5:** 10, 22, 32; white **1:** 21, 26-27, 30, 34, 36-37, 46

blood pressure **1:** 9, 18-19, **4:** 25, 26, **5:** 43, **8:** 20, 33, 46

body temperature **1:** 22-23, **3:** 30, **6:** 10, 16-17, **8:** 12, 20, 33, 46

bone marrow **1:** 30-31, 46, **2:** 6, 12-13, 40, 46

bones **2:** 8, 10-11, 14-15, 40-41, 42-43; diseases **2:** 44-45; limbs **7:** 30, 32, 36; movement **2:** 30, **7:** 4, 6, 8, 24-25, 46; skull **2:** 16-17, 18-19, **7:** 28; tendons **7:** 12-13

brain **8:** 8-9, 20-21, 32-33, 34, 38, 46; cerebrum **8:** 24-25, 28-29, 30; damage **1:** 42, 44-45, **5:** 44; development **4:** 24, 38; energy **3:** 9, **7:** 35; motor control **7:** 6, 10-11, 20, 22, 29, 31, 33, **8:** 6, 18-19; neurons **8:** 6, 10-11, 19, 21; sensory areas **6:** 20-21, 22, 24, 28-29, 30; skull **2:** 8, 11, 16, 42; stem **2:** 19, 8: 21, 23, 36, 46; vision **6:** 32, 38-39, 40-41

breastbone see sternum

breasts **4:** 8, 40-41, **8:** 42

breathing **3:** 36-37, **5:** 8, 22, 26-27; control **8:** 8, 18, 20, 33, 46; organs **2:** 22, **5:** 20-21; rate **5:** 6, 24, 28-29, 43, **7:** 34

bronchi **5:** 10-11, 16-17, 18-19, 23, 34, 46; disease **5:** 34, 36, 38

C capillaries **1:** 8-9, 10-11, 23, 24, 26, 32, 46, **3:** 41, **5:** 22-23, 29, 46, **7:** 10, 14

cardiac (heart) muscle **1:** 13, 14, 19, 46, **7:** 6, 38, 40-41, 46

cartilage **2:** 14-15, 40, 46, **5:** 14, 16, 46, **6:** 22; baby **2:** 4, 14, 20; joints **2:** 12, 20-21, 27, 32-33, 34-35, 44; ribs **2:** 22-23

central nervous system (CNS) **8:** 8, 10-11, 46

cerebellum **8:** 4, 20-21, 26, 32-33, 34-35, 46

cerebrum **8:** 9, 19, 20-21, 32, 34, 46; cortex **6:** 8, 9, 32, 46, **8:** 22-23, 26, 28, 46; hemispheres **8:** 20, 22-23, 24-25

clavicle (collar bone) **2:** 8, 23, 25, 46

consciousness **5:** 42, 46, **8:** 18-19, 20, 46

cornea **6:** 32, 34, 36, 43, 46

coronary arteries **1:** 18-19, 44, 46, **7:** 35

D dendrites **6:** 9, **8:** 10-11, 15

diaphragm **2:** 22, **5:** 10-11, 20, 26, 46

digestive system **3:** 6-7, 10-11, 12-13, 30-31, 32, **7:** 35, 38, **8:** 41, 46; control **8:** 33, 39; intestines **3:** 20-21, 22-23, 26-27; stomach **3:** 18-19;

E ears **2:** 16, 18, **6:** 6, 22-23, 24-25, 26, 46, **7:** 10, 20; balance **6:** 28, **8:** 35

eggs see ova

embryo **4:** 19, 20-21

endocrine system **1:** 23, 46, **8:** 6, 33, 40-41, 42-43, 46

energy **7:** 34-35, 41, 46; food **3:** 6, 8-9, 28, 34, 46; metabolism **5:** 8-9, 46, **7:** 6, 16-17, 18

enzymes **3:** 10-11, 30-31, 46; gastric **3:** 18-19; intestinal **3:** 20-21, 22, **8:** 41, 46; saliva **3:** 12-13

esophagus (gullet) **3:** 11, 13, 16-17, 18, 46, **5:** 14, **7:** 6, 39

exercise **1:** 18, **2:** 21, 31, **3:** 8, **7:** 34-35, 36-37, 40, 42, 44

eyes **2:** 18, **4:** 36-37, **6:** 6, 32-33, 34, 36-37, 38-39, 40, 42-43, **8:** 12, 35, 38

F face **2:** 6, 16, 18-19, **4:** 21, 22, 24, **7:** 28-29

fallopian tube **4:** 9, 11, 16-17, 18, **7:** 39

fertilization **4:** 10, 12, 16-17, 30, 34-35

femur (thigh bone) **2:** 6, 9, 10-11, 26-27, 28-29, 32, 35, 40, 46, **7:** 32; blood cells **1:** 31, **2:** 12

fertilization **4:** 16-17, 30-31, 32, 34-35

fetus **4:** 6, 21, 22-25, 26, 30

fibula **2:** 9, 28-29, 46

foot **2:** 9, 11, 15, 28-29, 38, 46, **7:** 32-33, **8:** 35

G gall bladder **3:** 11, 20-21, 22, 25, 46

genes **4:** 30-31, 32-33, 36-37

glands **1:** 34, 46, **3:** 27, 30, 46, **8:** 38-39; digestive **3:** 6, 12-13, 18-19, **8:** 40; endocrine **8:** 36, 40-41, 42-43, 44, 46; mammary **4:** 8, 40-41, **8:** 42; sweat **6:** 13, 16-17, **8:** 39, 40; tear **6:** 33

gray matter **8:** 14-15, 22-23, 46

H hair **3:** 29, **4:** 22-23, 40-41, 42-43, 44, **6:** 10, 12-13, 16-17, 20, 22

hand **2:** 6, 11, 24-25, 30-31, 34, 38, 44, 46, **7:** 12, 30-31

hearing **6:** 6, 22, 24-25, 26-27, **8:** 23, 32

heart **1:** 6, 10, 12-13, 46, **7:** 40-41; beat **1:** 14-15, 16-17, 18-19, 46, **5:** 28, 43; control **8:** 8, 18, 20, 33, 38-39, 46; disease **5:** 36; exercise **3:** 9, **7:** 34-35,

36-37; respiration **5:** 10, 18, 22; ribs **2:** 8, 11, 22-23

heart muscle see cardiac muscle

hemoglobin **1:** 24, 46, **3:** 33, **5:** 10, 46

hip bones see pelvis

hormones **1:** 22-23, 46, **4:** 10, 14-15, 26, 41, 43, **8:** 6, 40-41, 42-43, 44-45, 46

humerus **1:** 31, **2:** 8, 25, 36-37, 40-41, 46, **7:** 13

I ilium **2:** 26-27, 46

immune system **1:** 36-37, 38-39, 46

intestines **1:** 10-11, 22-23, **2:** 26, **7:** 6, 38; large **3:** 6, 26-27; small **3:** 18, 20, 26, 30-31

iris **6:** 32-33, 34, 46, **8:** 38

ischium **2:** 26-27, 46

J jaws **2:** 17, 18-19, 42, **3:** 12-13, 14-15, **5:** 15, **7:** 25, 46

joints **2:** 9, 16, 27, 32-33, 38-39, 44, 46, **7:** 8, 24-25, 31, 36, 46; ball-and-socket **2:** 24-25, 30-31, 32, 36-37; cartilage **2:** 12, 14; hinge **2:** 29, 32, 34-35

K kidneys **1:** 10, 22, **3:** 8-9, 38-39, 40-41, 46, **7:** 35

knee **2:** 10, 28-29, 32, 34-35, 44

L larynx (voice box) **4:** 42-43, **5:** 10-11, 14-15, 46

legs **1:** 10, **2:** 10, 28-29, 31, 43; muscles **7:** 9, 11, 12, 20-21, 26, 32-33, 46

ligaments **2:** 12, 32, 34-35, 36, 46

liver **3:** 6, 9, 22, 24-25, 46, **7:** 35; circulation **1:** 10, 22 23, 30; digestion **3:** 11, 20-21, 30, 46

lungs **5:** 10-11, 16-17, 18-19, 46; baby **4:** 28, **5:** 24; breathing **5:** 8, 20-21; circulation **1:** 10, 16-17, 22, 24; disease **5:** 34, 36-37, 38-39; gas exchange **5:** 22-23; ribs **2:** 8, 11, 22-23

lymphatic system **1:** 26, 32-33, 34-35, 36, 46

lymphocytes **1:** 9, 21, 26-27, 30, 34, 46; immunity **1:** 36-37, 38

M macrophages **1:** 33, 34-35, 36, 46, **5:** 34, 36

memory **6:** 20, 40, **7:** 31, **8:** 22, 26, 28-29, 30, 32, 36, 46

menstrual cycle (period) **4:** 10-11, 40-41, 44

motor nerves **6:** 8, 14-15, 46 **7:** 11, 20-21, **8:** 6, 8, 10, 14-15, 16-17, 25, 46

mouth **3:** 6, 10-11, 12-13, 30-31; breathing **5:** 11, 12-13, 15

mucus **6:** 32-33, 46; airways **5:** 6, 12-13, 17, 34, 36, 38, 40, **6:** 20-21; gut **3:** 13, 16, 18-19, 23, 26-27

muscle fibers (cells) **1:** 11, 22-23, **7:** 4, 6, 8-9, 10-11, 14-15, 46; **8:** 13, 16, 46; cardiac **1:** 12, 14, 16, 18, 46, **7:** 40-41; contraction **7:** 16-17, 18, 20-21, 26, 46; smooth **7:** 38

muscles **2:** 8, 10, 22, 30-31, 34, **3:** 46, **4:** 22, 44, **7:** 14-15; body **2:** 18-19, 24-25, 12-13, **7:** 6, 8-9, 10-11, 24-25, 26-27, 35, 37, 42-43, 44-45, 46; control **6:** 15, 30, **8:** 8, 10, 17, 22-23, 35, 38-39; internal organs **3:** 10, 16-17, 18, 22, 26, 42-43, **4:** 26, 28, **5:** 10, 16, 20, 40, 42, 46, **6:** 32-33, 34-35; metabolism **3:** 9, **5:** 28-29, **7:** 16-17, 18-19

N nerve cells see neurons

nerve fibers see axons

nerve signals **2:** 18, **6:** 8, 22, 24, 32, **7:** 11, 16, 20-21, 23, 41, 46, **8:** 12-13, 46

nerves **7:** 12, 20, 21, **3:** 14, **7:** 16, 20-21, 40, 46

nervous system **6:** 8-9, **7:** 20, 38, 40, **8:** 8-9

neurons (nerve cells) **6:** 8, 9, **7:** 6, 11, 20-21, 46, **8:** 6, 8-9, 10-11, 13, 46; brain **8:** 21, 22, 25; spinal cord **6:** 4, 8, 14-15, 46, **8:** 14
nose **2:** 14, 17, 18-19, **3:** 16, **5:** 10-11, 12-13, 34, 38, 40, 46, **6:** 6, 20-21
nutrients **1:** 22-23, **3:** 8, 10, 22-23, 24-25, 34, **5:** 8, 46

O olfactory nerves **5:** 12, **6:** 20-21, **8:** 32
optic nerves **6:** 33, 34, 37, 38-39
ova (eggs) **4:** 6, 8-9, 10-11, 32, 44, **8:** 40-41; fertilization **4:** 16-17, 18, 30-31, 34-35, 37
ovaries **4:** 6, 8-9, 32, 41, 44, **8:** 40-41; ovulation **4:** 10-11, 30-31

P pain **6:** 6, 10, 12-13, 14-15, **8:** 17, 22, 32
pancreas **3:** 11, 20-21, 22, 30, 46, **8:** 41, 43, 46
parasympathetic nervous system **8:** 8, 38-39
patella (knee cap) **2:** 9, 10, 28-29, 32, 46
pelvis (hips) **2:** 6, 9, 10, 26-27, 36, 44, 46, **4:** 9, 10, 40, **7:** 32-33; blood cells **1:** 31
penis **3:** 39, **4:** 12-13, 14, 16, 42
period see menstrual cycle
peristalsis **3:** 10, 17, 22, 46, **7:** 39
pharynx (throat) **3:** 13, 16-17, **5:** 10, 12-13, 14, 34, 38
pineal gland **8:** 36
pituitary gland **4:** 10, 14, 26, **8:** 40-41, 42, 46
placenta **4:** 19, 24, 26, 28, 30-31, **5:** 24
plasma **1:** 20, 22-23, 28, 37, 46
platelets **1:** 20-21, 26-27, 28, 30, 46
pregnancy **4:** 10, 24-25, 26, 30
puberty **4:** 8, 40-41, 42-3
pulmonary vessels **1:** 10, 12, 14-15, 16, **5:** 18-19
pupil **6:** 32-33, 34, 45, 46, **8:** 16, 33, 38

R radius **2:** 25, 41, 46, **7:** 13
red blood cells **1:** 6, 8, 20-21, 22, 24-25, 46, **3:** 24, 33, **5:** 10, 22, 32; blood groups **1:** 40-41; clotting **1:** 28-29; manufacture **1:** 30, **2:** 12
reflex action **3:** 16, **6:** 8, 14-15, **8:** 14, 16-17, 46
reproductive system **4:** 6, 8-9, 12-13, 40-41, 42-43, **7:** 39
respiration **1:** 22, **5:** 8-9, 22
respiratory system **5:** 10-11, 24, 26, 34
retina **6:** 34-35, 36-37, 42-43, 45, 46
ribs **1:** 12, **2:** 8, 10, 13, 21, 22-23, 46, **5:** 10-11, 18, 20

S sacrum **2:** 20, 26-27
saliva **3:** 10, 12-13, 36, **6:** 18, 46, **8:** 38-39, 40
scapula (shoulder blade) **2:** 8, 25, 36-37, 46
scrotum **4:** 12-13, 14, 42
secondary sexual characteristics **4:** 41, 43, **8:** 41
semicircular canal **6:** 22, 28-29, 30, 46, **8:** 35
senses **2:** 16, **4:** 24, **6:** 4, 8-9, 22, **8:** 8, 10, 12, 14-15, 17, 46
sexual intercourse **4:** 12, 16-17
shin bone see tibia
shoulder **2:** 24-25, 31, 32, 36-37, **7:** 8-9, 24, 31
skeletal (voluntary) muscles **7:** 6, 8-9, 10-11, 42, 46; control **7:** 20, **8:** 16, 46; movement **7:** 26-27, 34; structure **7:** 14-15
skeleton **2:** 6, 8-9, 10-11, 14, 46, **4:** 21, **7:** 4
skin **4:** 25, 40-41, 42, 44, **6:** 6, 10-11, 12-13, 16-17, 30, **7:** 28-9, 35, **8:** 10, 12, 17, 35
skull **2:** 6, 8, 10-11, 46; blood cells **1:** 31, **2:** 13; cranium **2:** 16-17, 42-43, **8:** 6, 19; face **2:** 18-19, **6:** 32, **7:** 28; joints **2:** 32, 38-39
sleep **5:** 28, **7:** 26, **8:** 18, 33, 36-37, 40
smell **5:** 12, **6:** 6, 18, 20-21, **8:** 23, 26, 32
smooth muscle **3:** 10, 22, **7:** 6, 38-39

speech **5:** 14, **8:** 23
sperm **4:** 4, 6, 12-13, 14-15, 42-43, 44, **8:** 40-41
spinal cord **2:** 11, 19, 20-21, 46, **6:** 4, 8, 14-15, 46, **7:** 20, 46, **8:** 6, 8-9, 14-15, 16-17, 46
spine **2:** 8-9, 10, 20-21, 22-23, 26-27, 38-39, 44-45, 46, **8:** 14-15
sternum (breastbone) **1:** 31, **2:** 8, 22-23, 46
stomach **3:** 6, 10-11, 18-19, 30-31, 44, 46
striped (striate) muscle **7:** 8-9, 14, 16
swallowing **3:** 16-17, **5:** 14, **7:** 6
sweat **3:** 36-37, 42, **4:** 40-41, 42, **6:** 11, 12-13, 16-17, 20, **7:** 18, **8:** 39, 40
sympathetic nervous system **8:** 8, 38-39
synapse **6:** 9, **7:** 21, **8:** 12-13, 46

T taste **3:** 4, 12-13, **6:** 6, 18-19, 20, 46, **8:** 23, 32
teeth **2:** 18, 42, **3:** 14-15, 44, **4:** 22, **5:** 15; digestion **3:** 6, 10-11, 12-13
tendons **2:** 10, 12, 24, 28, 32, 34, 46, **6:** 30, **7:** 12-13, 30, 32, 40, 46; disorders **7:** 42-43, 44-45
testes **4:** 4, 12-13, 14-15, 32, 42-3, **8:** 40, 41
thigh bone see femur
throat see pharynx
thyroid gland **8:** 40, 42
tibia (shin bone) **2:** 9, 28-29, 32, 35, 41, 46
tongue **3:** 4, 12-13, 16-17, **5:** 14-15, **6:** 6, 18-19, 46
tonsils **1:** 33, 34
touch **6:** 6, 10-11, 12-13, 14, **8:** 23, 32, 35
trachea (windpipe) **2:** 14, **3:** 16-17, **5:** 6, 10-11, 13, 16-17, 18-19, 46
triceps muscle **2:** 34, **7:** 11, 13, 16, 22-23, 25
twins **4:** 30-31, 36

U ulna **2:** 8, 25, 41, 46, **7:** 13
umbilical cord **4:** 22, 24, 28-29, **5:** 24
urine **1:** 22, **3:** 24, 36-37, 38-39, 46, **8:** 40; system **3:** 40-41, 42-43, **4:** 8-9, 13, **7:** 38
uterus (womb) **2:** 26, **4:** 6, 8-9, 10-11, 40, **5:** 24; birth **4:** 26, 28, **7:** 39; pregnancy **4:** 16-17, 18- 19, 22-23

V vagina **4:** 8-9, 10-11, 12, 16-17, 28
valves   heart **1:** 12-13, 14-15, 16-17, 46; lymph ducts **1:** 32-33; veins **1:** 9
veins **1:** 8-9, 10-11, 22, 24, 46, **3:** 25, 41; respiratory system **5:** 18-19, 23
vena cava **1:** 9, 12, 14-15, 46
vertebrae **2:** 8-9, 20-21, 22, 32, 45, 46, **7:** 25, 27, **8:** 14; blood cells **1:** 31, **2:** 13
vision **6:** 32-33, 40-41, 42-43, 44, 45, **8:** 23, 26; brain **6:** 32, 38-39
voice box see larynx
voluntary muscles see skeletal muscles
vulva **3:** 39, **4:** 8-9

W waste **3:** 9, 24, 38, 40; digestive tract **3:** 11, 23, 26-27, 32, 46
water balance **3:** 26-27, 36-37, 38-39
white blood cells **1:** 20-21, 26-27, 28, 30-31, 46
white matter **8:** 14-15, 22-23, 46
windpipe see trachea
womb see uterus
wrist **2:** 9, 24-25, 31, 32, 38, 46

Acknowledgments

The publishers wish to thank the following for supplying photographs:
Dr. Jeremy Burgess/Science Photo Library (SPL) 11 (BR), 17 (TL); BSIP DuCloux/SPL 21 (BR); BSIP Vem/SPL 6 (CR), 20 (BL); Scott Camazine/SPL 11 (B); Prof. S. Cinti, Universite d'Ancone, CNRI/SPL 6 (TL), 18 (BL); CNRI/SPL front cover (TL), 25 (TL), 3 (CR), 12 (BL), 9 (BL), 39 (B); Custom Medical Stock Photo/SPL 37 (BR); Martin Dohrn/SPL 17 (BL); Eye of Science/SPL 44 (B), 45 (B); Eric Grave/SPL 13 (CR); Manfred Kage/SPL 2 (CR), 10 (TL), 13 (TR), 15 (TR); Bill Longcore/SPL 37 (TL); Damien Lovegrove/SPL 24 (B); Astrid and Hanns-Frieder Michler 14 (TL); Miles Kelly Archives 4 (TR), 14 (CL), 17 (CL, CR), 19 (C), 26 (TL, C, B), 27 (TL, TR), 30 (TR), 36 (C, B), 38 (B), 40 (R), 41 (C, BL), 44 (TR), 45 (TL, C, TR); Prof. P. Motta/Dept. of Anatomy/University "La Sapienza," Rome/SPL front cover (CR, BL), 6 (CL), 32 (BR), 33 (BR), 25 (BR), 19 (CL, BL), 23, 35 (TR), 36 (TL); Profs. P. Motta and A. Caggiati/University "La Sapienza," Rome/SPL 24 (BL), 31; Panos 28 (TL), 30 (BL); D. Phillips/SPL 6 (B); Quest/SPL 10 (BL), 11 (T), 15 (CR); Secchi-Lecaque/Roussel-UCLAF—CNRI/SPL 15 (BL), 21 (TL); Pat Spillane 8 (BL, model Puspita McKenzie), 10 (C), 14 (B), 20 (TL, model Shoji Tanaka), 22 (TL, model Laura Saunter), 28 (B, model Shoji Tanaka), 29 (TR, model Wesley Stevenson), 42 (B, model Tom Saunter); The Stock Market 24 (TL); Gary Watson/SPL 14 (BL); Richard Wehr/SPL 17 (TR).